TWILIGHT OF THE EMPIRE

THE ROMAN INFANTRYMAN 3RD TO 6TH CENTURY AD

Text by
SIMON MACDOWALL
Colour plates by
GERRY EMBLETON

First published in Great Britain in 1994 by
Osprey Publishing, Elms Court, Chapel Way,
Botley, Oxford OX2 9LP United Kingdom
Email: info@ospreypublishing.com

Also published as Warrior 9 *Late Roman Infantryman*
236-565AD

ISBN 1 84176 112 5

Filmset in Great Britain
Printed in China through World Print Ltd.

FOR A CATALOGUE OF ALL BOOKS PUBLISHED BY
OSPREY MILITARY AND AVIATION
PLEASE WRITE TO:

The Marketing Manager, Osprey Direct USA, PO Box 130,
Sterling Heights, MI 48311-0130, USA.
Email: info@ospreydirectusa.com

The Marketing Manager, Osprey Direct UK, PO Box 140,
Wellingborough, Northants, NN8 4ZA, United Kingdom.
Email: info@ospreydirect.co.uk

Visit Osprey at:
www.ospreypublishing.com

Dedication
To Gabriele, Katharina and Alexander

Acknowledgements
Many thanks to Kim Reid and David Nicolle for the
line drawings; and Bernd Lehnhoff, Theodore
Adamakopoulos and Dimitris Christodoulou for
providing me with valuable source material and
advice.

FRONT COVER: Sarcophagus, 180-190 AD
(photograph courtesy of Kalervo Koskimies)

BACK COVER: Courtesy of Simon MacDowall

HISTORICAL BACKGROUND

The late Roman *pedes*, or ordinary infantryman, was probably not a Roman at all and may even have had difficulty speaking any recognisable form of Latin. He was probably a German, but he could equally have been an Isaurian from the mountains of Asia Minor, or from anywhere inside or outside the borders of the Roman world. He lived and fought in one of the most tumultuous and significant periods in the history of Europe.

Between the 3rd and 6th centuries AD, the traditional legions of heavy infantry were whittled away and eventually replaced by a force of various arms and nationalities, dominated by cavalry and supported by missile troops. However, in spite of this trend towards cavalry, the *pedes* remained the backbone of the Roman army until well into the 5th century. The *pedes* was different from the legionary who preceded him; perhaps he was not as well disciplined, but in many ways he was more flexible – ready for rapid deployment to trouble spots, and for fighting both as a skirmisher and a heavy infantryman. This book looks at who this man was and how he lived and fought.

Reorganisation in the 3rd century

During the 3rd century AD, the Roman army made and unmade emperors at the drop of a hat, plunging the Empire into a vicious cycle of civil war and economic decline. Inflation, currency devaluation, unemployment and all the associated ills that we attribute to modern society were well known to the 3rd-century inhabitants of the Roman Empire. They were also subject to increasing pressures on the frontiers, as those people beyond the borders looked with envy at the apparent riches of those within.

The Roman Empire would probably have collapsed had it not been for a series of soldier-emperors from Illyria (an area roughly corresponding to the former Yugoslavia). These men, commanding soldiers raised in the same region, managed to secure the frontiers and bring about a degree of stability. Diocletian (AD 284–305) undertook a massive polit-

The Emperor Diocletian, who was responsible for a complete overhaul of the Imperial administration, depicted with his co-rulers. They are wearing the pillbox style caps which seem to have been universal undress headgear for all ranks of the late Roman army. (Piazza San Marco, Venice)

ical reorganisation that split the Empire into eastern and western halves and stabilised the economy by freezing wages and prices. This reform of the Empire resulted in changes to nearly all aspects of life, including the military.

The new army that emerged from this reorganisation bore little resemblance to that which had preceded it. It was designed to provide a defence in depth: static troops of reduced status manned the frontiers, while field armies of new, smaller, more flexible units were held in reserve, ready to respond to sudden threats. We have a fairly good idea of how the army was organised from the *Notitia Dignitatum* which lists all army units for both halves of the Empire at the close of the 4th century AD.

At the core of the new army were the *comitatenses* – regional field armies based in central locations. They were formed partly by withdrawing some detachments from the frontier and partly by raising new units. Later, some elite units were classed as *palatini* and formed the Emperor's central field army. Before long, units of *comitatenses* and *palatini* became mixed in the same armies, although the *palatini* continued to have higher status.

Frontier forces, descendants of the old legions and auxiliaries, dropped in status and became stationary garrison troops known as *limitanei* (guarding the frontier zones – *limes*) or *ripenses* (based along river frontiers). Eventually these troops became little more than a part-time militia, and they were rarely called on to take part in major campaigns. When this did occur and *limitanei* were transferred to the field army, they were given the title *pseudocomitatenses*.

The new units created for the field armies were markedly smaller than the old 6,000-man legions: probably no more than 1000–1200 men. The majority

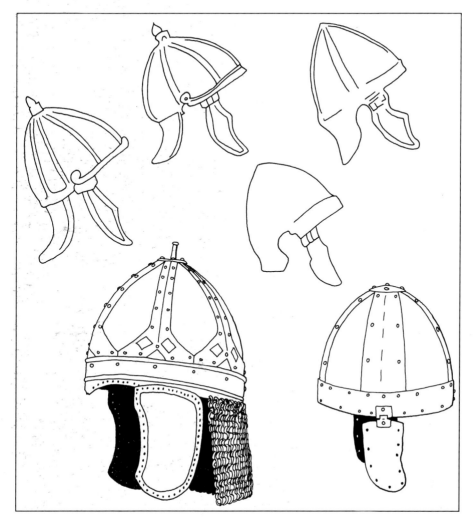

Spangenhelm *style helmets were worn before, during and after the late Roman period, both by Roman soldiers and their enemies. The top four are early Sarmatian and Roman examples (Trajan's column); bottom right is a very simple, crude 3rd-4th century version, perhaps mass produced (Rijksmuseum, Leiden); bottom left is a beautifully crafted 5th–6th century Gepid* spangenhelm *with chainmail neck guard.*

of the army's foot soldiers, however, were provided by new-style units called *auxilia*, which had an establishment strength of about 500 men. As is the case in all armies, actual strengths were probably much lower, particularly on campaign.

The old distinction of legionaries being citizens and auxiliaries non-citizens disappeared with the general enfranchisement of all inhabitants of the Empire in AD 212. Furthermore, by the 4th century AD both legions and *auxilia* were accepting recruits from beyond the Empire's borders – primarily Germans. At the Battle of Strasbourg (AD 357), the *Cornuti*, *Bracchiati*, and *Batavi* (all *auxilia*) are described fighting in the main line of battle alongside the *Primani* legion. They were apparently all wearing armour and fighting with spears, javelins and swords.

The 5th-century writer Flavius Vegetius Renatus says that the legions were more heavily equipped and more strictly disciplined than the *auxilia*. It may be that the *auxilia*, all of whom were higher status *palatini*, were trained to operate with a greater degree of flexibility than the legions: one day acting in small units in commando-style raids, the next day brigaded together in a larger formation, fighting in the line of battle. While there is no conclusive proof of this, contemporary writings suggest that whenever a tough job came up, the generals turned to the *auxilia palatina* to find their men. An indication that the legions were not this flexible can be found in an incident at the siege of Amida in AD 359, where two legions are described as being excellent fighters in open country 'but quite useless, indeed a positive nuisance' in more specialised operations.

Both legions and *auxilia*, therefore, should be looked upon as heavy infantry, performing basically the same task on the battlefield and being similarly equipped. The writings of Vegetius, however, imply that a portion of the men in each unit – legions and *auxilia* – were trained as light infantrymen. This is borne out in battle descriptions, where groups of skirmishers are usually formed by selecting men from various units, rather like 18th century light companies.

There were also a number of specialist light infantry such as *sagittarii* (archers), *exculcatores* (probably javelinmen), *funditores* (slingers) and *balistarii*. The *balistarii* are normally assumed to be artillerymen who manned small field catapults. While this is a logical assumption on the basis of their name, the one example we have of them in action sees them escorting a general and acting as skirmishers. An alternative explanation is that they were light infantry crossbowmen. In spite of the view that the crossbow was a medieval weapon, late Roman crossbows are known to have existed from archaeological finds, further supported by Vegetius who mentions troops 'who annoyed the enemy with arrows from the *manubalistae* or *arcubalistae*'.

A 3rd century Roman infantryman with German captive. For much of the mid-3rd century the situation might have been reversed. The soldier is wearing a muscled cuirass, probably an artistic convention to give him a more classical appearance. (Arch of Diocletian, Rome)

The head of a draco standard, probably adopted from the Sarmatians. It had an attached windsock body and was carried by a senior soldier called a draconarius. (Staatliches Amt für Vorund Frühgeschichte, Koblenz)

As the cavalry increased in importance in the 5th and 6th centuries, the infantry began to decline. Writing when Roman fortunes were at their lowest ebb, Vegetius says that 'the name of the legion remains to this day in our armies, but its strength and substance are gone'. While this degradation of the infantry may have started earlier, the 4th century *pedes* was as capable as his predecessor of standing firm in the line of battle, even if he was no longer looked upon as the elite of the army.

CHRONOLOGY

Major battles in bold

AD 236–268	Franks, Alamanni and Goths overrun Rhine and Danube frontiers.
251	Roman army defeated by Goths at **Forum Terebronii**.
258–261	Persian War. Romans defeated at **Edessa**. Emperor Valerian captured.
268–280	Illyrian emperors restore the frontiers.
271–273	Aurelian's successful campaign against Palmyra.
284–305	Reign of Diocletian. Complete reorganisation of Imperial administration and military system.
312	Constantine defeats Maxentius at **Milvan Bridge**.
313	Edict of Milan brings recognition for Christianity.
324–337	Constantine sole Emperor. Construction of new capital at Byzantium (Constantinople).
337–350	Inconclusive war with Persia.
351	Constantius' Eastern army defeats the Western troops of the usurper Magnentius at **Mursa**.
355–360	Julian's successful campaign against the Franks and Alamanni in Gaul.
357	Roman victory over the Alamanni at **Strasbourg**.
362–364	Failed campaign against the Persians.
368–369	'Barbarian Conspiracy' of Saxons, Picts and Scots overrun Britain. Order restored by Theodosius.
378	East Roman army destroyed by Goths at **Adrianople**. Emperor Valens killed.
379–395	Reign of Theodosius. Some semblance of order restored.
394	Theodosius' Eastern army, including 20,000 Goths, defeats the Western army of Arbogast at **Frigid River**.
401–404	Inconclusive campaign of Stilicho against Alaric.
405–406	Vast German migration led by Radagaisus defeated by Stilicho at **Florence**.
406–410	Vandals, Suevi, Alans and Burgundians cross the frozen Rhine and overrun Gaul and Spain.
407	Roman troops leave Britain.

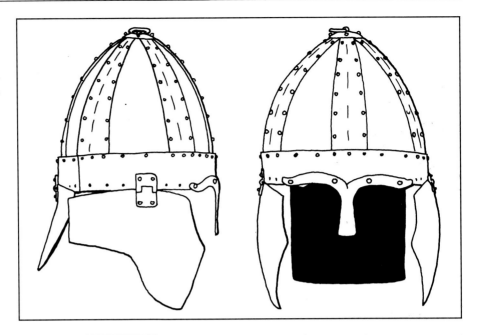

The figures below are based on soldiers from the Arch of Galerius. Both men wear the elaborate spangenhelm. The helmet shown on the right is based on a spangenhelm found at Der-el-Medineh Egypt.

410	Alaric sacks Rome.
419	Visigoths establish independent kingdom in southern Gaul.
421–422	Moderately successful campaign against Persia.
429	Vandals and Alans cross from Spain into Africa.
431	Failed joint East-West Roman campaign against Vandals in Africa.
433–450	Campaigns of Aetius against Visigoths, Franks and Burgundians in Gaul.
441–443	Hun invasion of the East. Romans defeated in the **Chersonese Peninsula**, Balkans ravaged. Romans agree to pay tribute.
447	Second Hunnic invasion of the East bought off by the Romans.
451	Hun invasion of the West checked by Aetius at **Chalons**.
455	The Vandals sack Rome.
476	Italian field army overthrows Emperor Romulus Augustulus. End of Western Empire.
492–496	Isaurian War. Primarily Gothic army under Anastasius defeats Isaurian partisans of Longinus.
507–512	Anastasius fortifies the frontiers against the Persians and Slavs.
524–531	Justinian's first war with Persia. Ends inconclusively.
532	Nika riots in Constantinople. 30,000 people die before order restored.
533–534	East Romans under Belisarius recover Africa from the Vandals.
534–554	Gothic War. A devastated Italy is restored to the Empire.
539–562	Justinian's second Persian War. Typically inconclusive.

RECRUITING

The 4th century army was considerably larger than its forerunners, at a time when the population of the Empire was in decline. Furthermore, soldiering was no longer considered an honourable or desirable profession, and it became increasingly difficult to find recruits to fill the ranks of this force, which on paper was over 500,000 strong.

The obligation to serve in the army passed from generation to generation. Sons of soldiers, including officers, were expected to serve unless physically unfit. Volunteers were used, and at times bounties were offered to attract them. Slaves were normally not allowed to join, but exceptions were made in crises. Senators and municipal officials were also barred from the army.

Hereditary and voluntary enlistment were not enough to fill the ranks, however, making an annual conscription necessary. The levy of conscripts was conducted in much the same way as the gathering of tax, with each village or estate being required to provide a set number of recruits. Providing recruits to the army was listed as one of the duties expected of landowners, along with the levying of pigs!

Military service was seemingly so unpopular that great lengths were taken to avoid it, including self-mutilation. Villagers would pay huge sums to local officials to avoid conscription, the officials in turn using the money to hire strangers to meet their quota, while making a profit on the side. Press gangs were occasionally employed to round up deserters and veterans' sons who were avoiding their duty.

New conscripts were supposed to be between 19 and 25 years old and physically fit. Sons of veterans, up to the age of 35, who had evaded service could be drafted. A minimum height requirement of 5ft. 7in. was recorded in AD 367, this seems rather tall considering the difficulty the authorities were having in filling the ranks. In the 5th century, the height requirement was abandoned as impractical.

In practice, the inspection of potential recruits was lax and we hear of complaints about landlords using the levy as an excuse to dump their least useful tenants on the army.

Once accepted, the recruit was given an identity disc and a certificate of recruitment. There are recorded instances of conscripts being branded on the hand or arm to identify them and make desertion more difficult. Desertion was certainly a problem, particularly amongst new recruits, and as a precau-

3rd century armoured infantrymen escorting the emperor. They are often taken to be cavalry since one man is leading the emperor's horse, but they are all clearly on foot and are most likely Illyrian legionaries or guardsmen. (Arch of Galerius, Thesaloniki)

tion draftees were locked up in prison each night while en route to their units.

An illuminating anecdote is described in the *Acta of Maximilanus*, the story of a Christian conscientious objector in Africa during the reign of Diocletian. Maximilanus was dragged before the Proconsul Dio proclaiming, 'I cannot serve, I cannot do evil. I am a Christian.' This apparently did not greatly impress the Proconsul, who ordered him tied up and measured. When his height was confirmed as 5ft. 10in. the Proconsul ordered, 'Let him be branded', and the reluctant Maximilanus found himself in the army.

Above: This well-preserved late Roman tunic from Egypt is made of an undyed wool-linen mix with indigo decorative patches sewn on. Most Roman soldiers of the period probably wore very similar tunics, although some may have dyed their tunics. There are no depictions of rank and file soldiers wearing square decorative patches. It is therefore possible that these were only worn by officers or civilians. (Städtisches Museum, Trier)

Right: These completely armoured 3rd–4th century infantrymen probably belong to a legion rather than an auxilia, assuming Vegetius is correct in saying that the legionaries had heavier arms. (Museo Chiaramonti, Vatican, after Coulston)

Hiring barbarians

The quality of soldiers recruited by conscription undoubtedly left a great deal to be desired, and would account for the fact that authorities looked more and more to foreigners to fill the ranks, not only of the auxiliary units but of all parts of the army, including the officer corps. By accepting money in lieu of a reluctant draftee, the army could hire a willing German instead. Such foreigners gave loyal service to the Empire, at least before the practice of hiring tribes *en masse* under their own leaders became commonplace.

Although many units, particularly in the new *Auxilia Palatina*, bore tribal names, there is no evidence to suggest that attempts were made to keep different nationalities in separate units. In fact the opposite seems to have been true, with barbarians and Romans fighting side by side in the same units and the numbers of Romans steadily decreasing as time went on. Foreigners could rise to very high rank, and by the mid 4th century many, and perhaps most, generals were of German or Sarmatian origin.

The system of individual recruitment apparently broke down in the aftermath of Roman defeats in Julian's Persian campaign (AD 363), and at the hands

of the Goths (AD 378). The ever-present problem of finding sufficient recruits could only have been made worse following the cumulative losses suffered in these campaigns. Furthermore, the prestige of Roman arms would have been significantly lowered, making potential German recruits think twice before enlisting.

The solution to this problem, as well as the problem posed by a marauding Gothic army in Roman territory, was to incorporate the Goths into the Roman army. A peace settlement was reached which granted the Goths the status of federates: giving them land in return for military service. This was to set the pattern for the 5th century, as the well of Roman and even individual German recruits dried up. Only 12 years after the settlement with the Goths, Emperor Theodosius took to the field with 20,000 of them to defeat a West Roman army commanded by a Frank and containing large numbers of Germans and Alans. After that, barbarians fighting under their own leaders formed the core of Roman field armies, especially in the west, until in AD 476 they did away with the puppet emperor and took control of their own affairs.

TRAINING

The new recruit, regardless of origin, was drafted into an existing unit; it was rare for new units to be raised entirely of recruits. The continuation of unit names from the 4th to the 6th century indicates that after suffering losses, units were recruited back up to strength rather than disbanded and replaced by new formations. Even many of the units created by Diocletian and Constantine can be traced back to the old legions. In normal circumstances, therefore, a recruit would take his place in the ranks beside veterans with up to 20 years experience who were a ready source of instruction and acted as role models for the recruit.

In addition to 'on the job training', the recruit was formally instructed in weapons handling and drilled in unit manoeuvre. As in all armies, training varied considerably, not only in time and place but also between units. Some units of *limitanei*, for example, were little more than part-time peasant militia, with soldiers running their own farms and becoming engaged in other trades. We hear, for

3rd century gravestone of Severius Acceptus, Legio VIII Augusta. *Roman tradition usually depicted unarmoured soldiers on gravestones, misleading some modern authors into thinking that soldiers of the period went into action without full equipment. (Archaeological Museum, Istanbul, after Coulston)*

example, of a devout Christian soldier in the 6th century who used to spend his days weaving baskets and praying, then at 3pm he went on parade with his unit. There are other examples of soldiers neglecting drill and becoming engaged in a variety of non-military activities, even cultivating the estates of powerful landowners. A variety of laws from the end of the 4th century indicate that the authorities tried to stop this – but apparently with little success.

A loss of discipline and neglect of training became common complaints of writers in the 5th century, and men such as Vegetius urged a return to the more vigorous training of former years. It is hard to say to what degree training was neglected, but the performance of field army units, particularly in the 4th century, shows a high degree of flexibility and proficiency that could only have been achieved with relatively thorough training.

Weapons training

Weapons handling was, perhaps, the first and most important skill to be taught to the new recruit. He was expected to become proficient with a variety of weapons and to use them in different situations. The late Roman *pedes* in the better field army units, particularly the *auxilia palatina*, could be employed as both a hand-to-hand fighter and a skirmisher. Vegetius places great emphasis on multiple weapons training, and while he mixes up his perception of what was done in the past with what he proposes for the future, we get some interesting glimpses of how weapons training might have been conducted in the 5th century.

The heavy infantryman was taught to use the spear (*lancea*), sword (*spatha*), javelins *(veruta)* and darts (*mattiobarbuli* or *plumbatae*). According to the *Strategikon* (a 6th century military manual), the infantryman 'should be trained in single combat against others, armed with shield and staff, also in throwing the short javelin and the lead weighted dart a long distance'. Vegetius mentions training with darts, and that the soldier should carry five of them in the hollow of his shield: 'thus the legionary soldiers seem to supply the place of archers, for they wound both men and horses of the enemy before they come into range of the common missile weapons [javelins]'.

In order to increase strength and accuracy, Vegetius recommends that recruits 'be furnished

Insignia of the Magistri Officiorum *from the* Notitia Dignitatum *showing their responsibility for the* fabricae, *or state arms factories. (Bodleian Library, Oxford)*

with javelins of greater weight than common' and be taught to throw them 'with proper aim and force'. When throwing javelins, the soldier would have his left leg forward, he would then draw his sword and take a step forward with his right foot to increase his reach.

Vegetius also tells us that between a third and a quarter of the recruits should be trained as archers. It is one thing, however, to train a heavy infantryman to operate as a skirmisher with weapons similar to those he is already familiar with, but quite a different thing to introduce weapons training that requires completely new skills. It would also have caused immense logistical difficulties to keep different sets of weapons and ammunition within the same relatively small unit. It is unlikely, therefore, that each unit would have maintained any integral archers on its strength. It is far more likely that from any batch of new recruits, those with talent or experience were selected

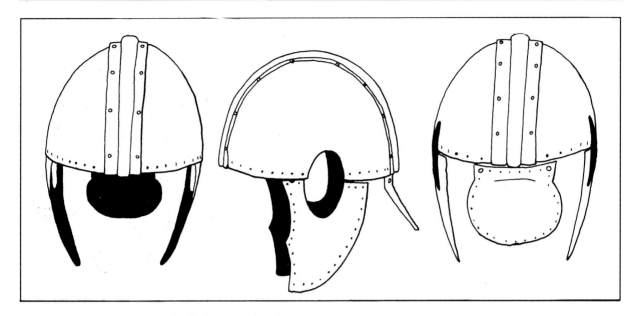

This simple ridge helmet was probably mass produced by the fabricae. The holes along the edges were to attach a leather lining. Cheek pieces and back plate were laced to the main bowl. Additional plates possibly covered the large ear holes. (August, Germany, after James)

for training as archers and then posted to specialised archery units, of which many are listed in the *Notitia Dignitatum*, particularly in eastern armies. It is interesting to note that the ratio of archer units to other *auxilia* in the main eastern armies was 1:5, fairly close to Vegetius' proportions.

However they were organised, it is clear from all sources that archer units would have been trained and tactically employed together with the heavy infantry. The *Strategikon*, for example, says 'at present we form the archers and others with missiles behind the files for drill'.

Drill

It is unclear how much drill, physical fitness or marching was included in the training of the late Roman soldier. Vegetius laments that such exercises were being neglected, but to what degree probably varied considerably between units. Drill in the 6th century is described in the *Strategikon*. It begins with the command, '*Silentium. Mandata captate. Non vos turbatis. Ordinem Servate. Bando sequite. Nemo demittat bandum et inimicos seque.*' (Silence. Observe orders. Do not worry. Keep your position. Follow the standard. Do not leave the standard and pursue the enemy.) The soldiers had to learn to respond to commands by voice, hand signal and trumpet so as not to be confused by the din of battle. They were trained to advance in silence while maintaining their alignment.

Infantry drill seems to have been aimed at getting the men to increase or reduce the frontage of their formation by halving or doubling ranks. 'They should become accustomed to these movements, so that at a spoken command, a nod, or some other signal, they march or halt, reduce or divide the depth of the files, march steadily in close order for a good distance over various kinds of terrain, close or tighten their ranks in depth and width, march in *fulcum* [similar to the old *testudo* with shields covering their heads], and engage in mock battle, sometimes using staffs and sometimes naked swords.'

The drill and efficiency of the infantry probably declined over the 5th century, maintaining consistency with their changing role. Elite units continued to receive effective training but as time progressed these units were becoming fewer in number. Meanwhile, large portions of the army, that were only expected to serve as static garrisons, were given considerably less training and spent much of their time in non-military pursuits. Even the recommended training in the *Strategikon* is aimed at getting the infantry into their battle formation and then holding their position, rather than having them deliver any sort of decisive charge.

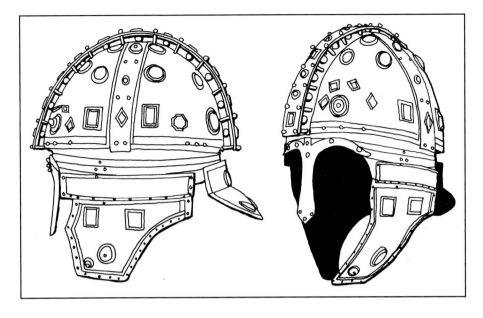

This magnificently decorated, elaborate ridge helmet is unlikely to have been worn by the rank and file except perhaps by one or two long-service soldiers with extra money to spare. (Berkasovo, Yugoslavia, after Junkelmann)

APPEARANCE AND EQUIPMENT

It is well known that the Roman army was equipped and supplied by the state. State run factories produced weapons, clothing and armour, the state provided rations and medical services, and it ran stud farms to raise cavalry mounts. The *Notitia Dignitatum* lists 35 state factories or *fabricae* across the Empire at the start of the 5th century, producing everything from catapults to armour. There were also state run clothing mills and boot makers.

It has been assumed, therefore, that the late Roman soldier was uniformly equipped, and modern reconstructions usually present such a view, even on campaign. Many modern authors have studied the available evidence and come up with theories on uniform distinctions for legions, cavalry and *auxilia* based on the assumption that all units of similar name would have the same uniform.

Such theories are probably grossly inaccurate: by the end of the 4th century, uniform issues were beginning to be replaced by a clothing allowance, and by the 6th century even weapons and armour were expected to be purchased by the soldiers from an allowance. A record from AD 423 states that five-sixths of the amount raised to clothe the army should go directly to the troops as a cash allowance, and only one-sixth be allocated to state clothing factories to produce uniforms for recruits.

Troops of the *limitanei* probably bought their clothing from stores attached to their fort. Even if such stores were furnished by state suppliers, we can assume that a certain amount of 'local flavour' would have crept into the soldiers' appearance. Since many soldiers in the 5th century *limitanei* had other occupations, it is unlikely that a high degree of uniformity could have been imposed on them once issue uniforms had been replaced by a clothing allowance.

It is generally assumed that the clothing of the field army would gave shown more consistency than that of the *limitanei*. However, because field units had no fixed base and were nearly always on campaign, regular supply from a fixed source would have been more difficult. In fact, the clothing allowance probably came about to ease the logistical difficulties of re-supplying these mobile troops. It is easy to picture such units after a long campaign presenting a very motley appearance; clothing does not last long in the field and the soldiers would have had to make local purchases fairly regularly

Taking as an example a unit of Julian's army assembled for the invasion of Persia, we can visualise them in Antioch, before they set off, presenting a fairly uniform appearance, at least within the unit. Even though the soldiers might have purchased their clothing themselves, chances are that a certain style would have predominated, even if colours and details varied according to individual taste and wealth. However, we would expect some of the veterans of Julian's Gallic army, having arrived in north European clothing, to have bought new clothes locally that were more suitable for the hot southern climate.

Once the campaign had begun, hot heavy items from the north would have been discarded. After the first few engagements, bits and pieces of Persian equipment would have started to appear: hacked shields, damaged helmets and armour would all have been replaced. On its return to Antioch, the army would have had a completely different appearance from when it left, and probably would have lost any semblance of uniformity. The same would hold true for almost any campaign, particularly those fought away from home.

The campaigns of the 5th century, in particular, were notorious for the participation of barbarian allies, and we can assume a fair deal of 'cross cultural' exchanges between the soldiers of different nationalities that served side by side. We would be very hard pressed indeed to distinguish between a 'Roman' soldier (perhaps born a Goth) serving in the army of Stilicho and a 'Gothic' soldier (perhaps born a Roman) in Alaric's army.

To identify such units in the field, the *Strategikon* says that shields should be of the same colour and it implies that helmet plumes were also in a uniform colour. Such simple details could provide a degree of uniformity.

The *Notitia Dignitatum* lists unit shield patterns in the same way as a modern equivalent might list unit cap badges. This does not guarantee that all men in the unit would have carried well-painted shields. After a battle, damaged shields would have been replaced from battlefield salvage or perhaps from a central reserve. It is highly unlikely that a soldier on campaign with such a replacement shield would have the time, or the paint, to reproduce some of the highly detailed designs shown in the *Notitia* before his next engagement. It is more likely that, at best, he would have given it a quick coat of paint in the official unit colour, leaving the job of fixing it up properly until after the campaign.

Armour

The question of how much armour was worn by the late Roman infantryman has been a matter of debate. Writing in the 5th century, Vegetius says,

'For though after the example of the Goths, the Alans and the Huns, we have made some improvements in the arms of the cavalry, it is plain that the infantry are completely exposed. From the foundation of the city until the reign of the Emperor Gratian [AD 367–383], the foot wore cuirasses and helmets. But negligence and sloth having by degrees introduced a total relaxation of discipline, the soldiers began to consider their armour too heavy and seldom put it on. They first requested leave from the Emperor to lay aside the cuirass and afterwards the helmet.'

Scale armour had a long tradition in the East and was worn by soldiers throughout the late Roman period. It was relatively easy to produce although it lacked the flexibility of mail. (Copyright British Museum)

Insignia of the Magistri Peditum, from a copy of the Notitia Dignitatum, showing shield designs of the senior western infantry units. (Bodleian Library, Oxford)

1 *Petulantes Seniores*
2 *Celtae Seniores*
3 *Ioviani Seniores*
4 *Herculiani Seniores*
5 *Divitenses Seniores*
6 *Tungrecani Seniores*
7 *Pannoniciani Seniores*
8 *Moesiaci Seniores*
9 *Armigeri Propugnatores Seniores*
0 *Lanciarii Sabariences*

11 *Octaviani*
12 *Thebaei*
13 *Cimbriani*
14 *Armigeri Propugnatores Iuniores*
15 *Cornuti Seniores*
16 *Brachiati Seniores*
17 *Heruli Seniores*
18 *Batavi Seniores*
19 *Mattiaci Seniores*
20 *Ascarii Seniores*
21 *Ascarii Iuniores*
22 *Iovii Seniores*

For further information on the shields of the late Roman Army see Men-at-Arms 247 Romano-Byzantine Armies.

Purple
Red
Blue
Yellow
Black
White
Green

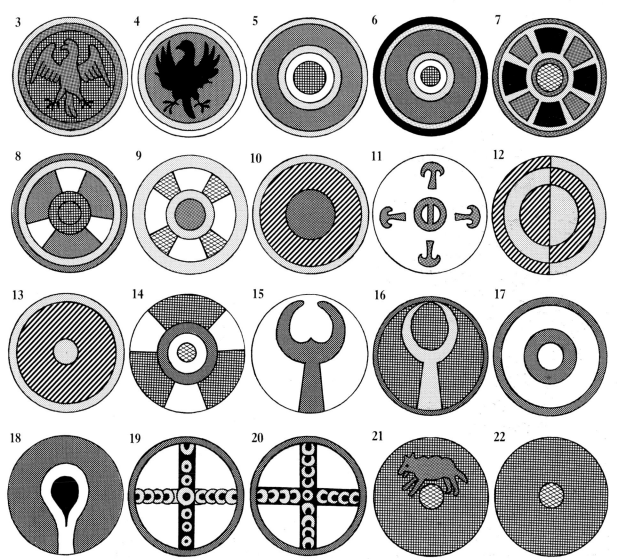

Both before and after Vegetius there is strong evidence that the Roman infantryman wore metal body armour and helmet. Ammianus Marcellinus, who was a soldier himself, makes frequent reference to 4th century infantry in 'gleaming' armour, and describes the infantry at Adrianople (AD 378) as 'weighed down by the burden of their armour'. Egyptian carvings from the 5th and 6th centuries clearly show Roman infantrymen wearing scale and mail armour. The 3rd century Arch of Galerius also shows infantrymen in scale armour.

Some monumental evidence appears to depict 3rd and 4th century infantry in leather muscled cuirasses. While it is possible that such armour was worn, it is far more likely to have been a classical convention employed by artists, and should not be taken at face value. There are numerous examples of artistic renditions of soldiers in heroic classical and pseudo-classical dress, continuing through to modern times. While leather muscled cuirasses may have been worn occasionally, archaeological and literary records indicate that iron mail or bronze scale was the most common body armour of the period.

Vegetius' claim that infantry armour was abandoned in the mid 4th century can be partially accounted for by the obvious material losses sustained in the Persian and Gothic disasters of the time. It is also consistent with the increase in use of federate troops and the introduction of allowances in place of issued equipment. If the main field armies of the 5th century were composed of barbarians and a few elite Roman cavalry units, it is quite likely that an infantryman would not have been willing to pay for expensive armour out of his allowance, nor have any real need for it. A large shield would probably have been sufficient protection for troops who only had a static supporting role.

For most of the soldier's service he would have no call to wear armour. Marches were conducted with armour carried in wagons, while routine guard duty, foraging expeditions and skirmishing no more called for armour than their modern equivalents call for the constant wearing of flak vests and helmets. Only when called on to fight in line of battle did the late Roman infantryman seem to need such added protection. The *Strategikon* calls for 'picked men ... to have mail coats, all of them if it can be done, but in any case the first two in the file'. This seems to imply that mail armour was kept in reserve rather than as part of an individual soldier's kit; it was issued as required. The same may even have been true of helmets, with soldiers usually wearing the characteristic pill-box shaped 'Pannonian leather cap' which Vegetius says was introduced to accustom the men 'to having the head covered so they might be less sensible of the weight of the helmet'.

It is difficult to say when, or to what degree, body armour for the infantry was re-introduced. It is quite probable that in some areas or units it never completely dropped out of use. Troops in richer

Iron link mail was probably the preferred defence for the late Roman soldier. Below is a sample of 6th century mail, now rusted together; right, a modern reconstruction. (Copyright British Museum)

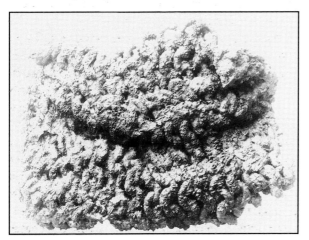

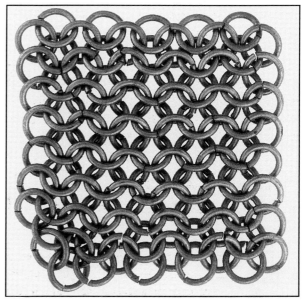

Gold neck torques deriving from pre-Roman Celtic traditions were often worn by late Roman soldiers. They were possibly a mark of rank or favour. They were worn by draconarii. *(Copyright British Museum)*

areas, in more stable posts, or in higher quality units may have used armour, while others abandoned it. This is consistent with the fact that most of the evidence for 5th and 6th century infantry armour comes from Egypt. Later Byzantine manuals all call for the infantry to be armoured, but whether such recommendations were always carried out is a matter of conjecture.

On balance, it seems reasonable to assume that the Roman infantryman until at least AD 378 wore metal body armour and a helmet when fighting in line of battle, whether he served in a legion or *auxilia*. When on patrol, on the march, on guard duty, or acting as a skirmisher, he probably left most of it off, as would specialist light infantry. The use of body armour may have become less common, as the role of infantry declined, but by the time of Justinian, at least some units were wearing full armour again, and its use probably never completely died out.

CONDITIONS OF SERVICE

A soldier normally served in the same unit for the duration of his career. On enrolment and during training he was considered a recruit (*tiro*), and he did not receive full pay and rations until fully integrated into his unit as a private (*pedes*). Service was normally for 20 years, but if the soldier served longer he received additional privileges and some significant tax exemptions for himself and his family. These included exemption from the poll tax as well as market and customs dues. He was also excused from civic duties, and this often led to the ruination of small landholders of the time. Like his predecessor in the earlier legions, the discharged veteran could expect a land grant. During the reign of Constantine, this included a pair of oxen, seed corn and a cash grant for expenses. The veteran could obtain a larger cash grant in lieu of land if he wished to go into business for himself, although this was discontinued in the 5th century.

Cross postings between units were rare. In AD 400, the general Stilicho reminded his commanders that such transfers could only be made with imperial authorisation. Promotion, therefore, was probably slow, as it would have been dependent on vacancies arising through casualty or retirement. This would have been particularly true in static units, where casualties would have been rare. The anonymous 4th century treatise *De Rebus Bellicis* complains that long-serving veterans blocked promotion and discouraged new recruits from joining up. One way around the problem was bribery. In a contract dated

The Column of Theodosius in Constantinople showing late Roman soldiers in undress uniform, wearing neck torques. (Author's photograph)

2 February AD 345, Aurelius Plas, a veteran, promises an officer, 'When you secure promotion in the name of my son ... whatever you give on account of said promotion, before God, as you give, I, Plas, will repay you in good faith in full.' The formality of such a contract indicates that such procedures were legal; or at least tolerated, and perhaps can be equated to the British army's system of purchasing commissions.

The rank structure in the new units of the late Roman army was quite different from that which preceded it. Units were commanded by a *tribunus*, assisted by a *vicarius*. For the *pedes*, the first step up was to *semissalis*. This was not a supervisory position, but rather a mark of experience. Then came the supervisory non-commissioned ranks which, in as-

cending order, included: *circitor, biarchus, centenarius, ducenarius, senator* and *primicerius*. In some cases a bright, experienced or well-connected soldier might be selected for the *protectores*, a sort of staff college that could lead to unit command. A particularly experienced soldier might also be appointed as the unit's *campidoctor*, or master at arms, responsible for drill and training – rather like a modern regimental sergeant major. Another experienced soldier would be appointed *draconarius* and carry the unit's windsock-style dragon standard (*draco*). Each unit also had a *medicus* to care for the sick and wounded, and by the end of the 5th century, when the army was thoroughly Christianised, units are also recorded as having chaplains on strength. Rounding out the supernumerary positions was the *bucinator* or trumpeter. The 6th century *Strategikon* also mentions armourers, weapons makers, bow makers and arrow makers.

Conditions, pay and rations

It is difficult to generalise about what life was like for the average soldier as conditions would certainly have varied considerably between units. Soldiers were allowed to marry, and their families were included on unit strength for rations. Pay, however, was usually provided in kind due to the general collapse of the economy and the high inflation of the 3rd century. Such payments included fairly generous issues of food and clothing, with increased allowances for higher rank. This was supplemented by regular cash donatives, paid from the imperial coffers on occasions such as the emperor's birthday and the anniversary of his ascension.

Rations seem to have been quite plentiful: a papyrus from Egypt gives a ration scale of 3lb of bread, 2lb of meat, 2 pints of wine and $\frac{1}{8}$ pint of oil per day. If this is neither exaggeration nor imaginative accounting, it means that Roman troops in Egypt were better fed than Americans in Britain during the Second World War! In any case meat, bread, oil and wine would have constituted the normal ration, perhaps with beer and butter rather than oil and wine in northern countries. The *limitanei* would have drawn rations from stores attached to the fort, while field army units would have had to resort to central warehouses or be fed by the town in which they were quartered. On campaign, a form of hard tack (*bucellatum*) was substituted for bread. This may be the origin of the nickname *bucellarii* which came to be applied to the personal retainers of 5th and 6th century warlords.

Although he had less status, fewer rations and lower pay, life for a soldier of the static *limitanei* was probably not too bad. Food and shelter were provided for him and his family, and he could expect to retire, tax exempt, to the family farm on discharge. He was recruited locally, his sons would serve in the same unit, and he would rarely, if ever, have to depart from home. On the other hand, he may never have had any cash pay and he had little, or no, opportunity for booty. Furthermore, since he might live on an isolated post, he was at the mercy of his commanders, who, if corrupt, might cut his rations and allowances to line their own pockets.

Many static garrison soldiers of the *limitanei*, and later the *comitatenses*, resorted to other occupations to produce an income. According to 6th century papers

Remnants of a 3rd century shield from Dura Europos. It is unlikely that such elaborate designs would have survived long on campaign. (Yale University Art Gallery)

from the family of Flavius Patermunthis (a soldier of the *limitanei*), the male members of the family were not only soldiers but also boatmen, carrying on fairly extensive business dealings and only limited military duties. Likewise, a soldier of the *Transtigritani* is recorded leasing a bakery from a soldier of the *Leones Clibanarii*.

Life in the mobile field army units would have been harder as the soldier had rarely the chance to settle down. Even these soldiers did not take kindly to moves that might remove them from their homeland forever. Thus Julian's Gallic army revolted and proclaimed their commander emperor, rather than obey an order from Constantius to move to the east. However, for the warlike soldier, there were compensations in the form of higher status and better pay and rations. It is quite probable that these units attracted a relatively high proportion of German adventurers who relished the prospects of action and booty, as opposed to a quiet life on the farm.

When not on campaign, field army soldiers were stationed in the cities of the interior. There were no permanent barracks so soldiers were quartered on the civilian population. A citizen was required to give up one third of his house to a soldier requiring accommodation. There was no reimbursement for this and there were many instances of soldiers bullying their reluctant hosts into providing them with food, fuel, bedding and even baths. This was not allowed by law, but with armed men on the doorstep the citizen had little recourse to the law.

An account by Joshua Stylites tells of troops at Edessa in AD 503 turning people out of their homes and stealing provisions. Other accounts tell of officers accepting money from a city so that their troops would not be billeted on them. Then, of course, there were incidents such as the soldier in AD 396 who married his landlady's daughter. When he was posted back to his home station, his new wife discovered he was already married and she became the first wife's slave. Justice eventually caught up with the man and he was sentenced to death, but many similar incidents are likely to have gone unrecorded.

THE SOLDIER ON CAMPAIGN

Most of the campaigns between the 3rd and 6th centuries were either civil wars or defensive campaigns against barbarian incursions. Two major exceptions to this were Julian's disastrous offensive against Persia in AD 363 and the brilliantly successful campaigns of Belisarius in the AD 530s.

On campaign with Belisarius

The infantryman played only a minor role in the campaigns of Belisarius. He might be tasked to garrison or lay siege to a city, but whenever serious fighting was called for it was the cavalryman who did the job. In fact, during the Gothic campaign, Procopius says that the 'regular infantry were now unwilling to remain in their accustomed condition, but, since they had captured horses as booty from the enemy and had become not unpractised in horsemanship, they were now mounted'. Becoming mounted infantry might have increased mobility, but it did little to improve their efficiency on the battlefield since Procopius goes on to say that they 'never had

The 4th century grave of Viatorinus killed by a Frank after 30 years service in 'barbarico'. At the time of his death he was a member of the protectores, a sort of staff college or corps of officer cadets through which a deserving veteran could rise to commissioned rank. (Römisch-Germanisches Museum, Cologne)

the courage to engage with the barbarians, but always turned to flight at the first onset'.

On one occasion, during the siege of Rome when Belisarius was planning to leave the infantry behind and engage the Goths with cavalry alone, two Isaurian officers pleaded with him to not be 'cut off from the infantry phalanx ... by means of which, as we hear, the power of the ancient Romans was brought to its present greatness'. They had to admit, however, that the infantry had 'done little of consequence in the war', and when they were reluctantly deployed well to the rear to act as a rallying point for the cavalry, they broke and ran on first contact.

The 4th century infantryman on campaign

The Roman infantry preparing for the invasion of Persia 130 years earlier are described by Ammianus Marcellinus as the 'flower of the army'. This campaign was the last time the Roman infantryman was called on to form the backbone of an army engaged in a strategic offensive.

To illustrate the life of a typical infantryman on campaign at this time, let us follow the exploits of a hypothetical soldier joining the *Petulantes, auxilium palatinum*, in France in AD 355 – the year that Julian

Shields were usually held by a central hand grip behind the boss, but some may have had an additional arm strap like this reconstruction. (Copyright British Museum)

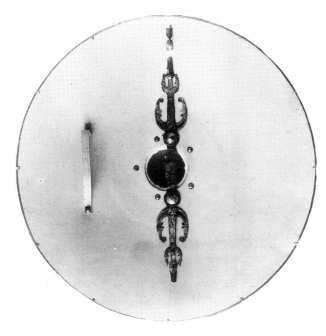

took command of the Gallic army. Our man probably came from the Gallic countryside, the population of which is described by Ammianus.

'*They are fit for service in war at any age ... their limbs are hardened by the cold and incessant toil, and there is no danger that they are not ready to defy. No one here ever cuts off his thumb to escape military service, as happens in Italy, where they have a special name for such malingerers (murci).*'

His unit was probably composed of such men together with any number of Germans, many of whom were already settled to the west of the Rhine. The total complement on paper was 500 men, but in order to form a larger tactical unit, the *Petulantes* were usually brigaded together with the *Celtae*. This brigading of units in pairs seems to have been very common: the *Petulantes* and *Celtae, Cornuti* and *Bracchiati, Joviani* and *Herculiani* – and many others – are almost always mentioned together, even at different times and places. Perhaps this indicates that a larger formation was used on campaign and that the smaller size of individual units was administrative rather than tactical.

On campaign against the Alamanni

Our soldier's first action may have been in AD 356. Starting out from Reims in a campaign to recover parts of north-western France from the Franks and Alamanni, Julian's troops marched 'in close order with unusual spirit'. The day was damp and grey 'so that it was difficult to see even at close range', when suddenly the two legions guarding the rear were ambushed. The attack was beaten off by auxiliaries who rushed to the legions' rescue, but for our man on his first campaign, a fierce skirmish in the fog must have been unnerving. His spirits probably improved, however, after a victory in a minor engagement near Brumath (in modern Alsace), particularly when this was followed by the recovery of several cities that had fallen to the Germans.

The soldier's life would then have settled into a routine of marches, sieges and the odd skirmish, but rarely a full blown battle. Food and rest were probably his first concerns, and were shared by his commander who 'devoted all his efforts to ensuring that after protracted toil his men should enjoy a period of rest'. Food was a perennial problem. Being constantly on the move, the troops of the mobile field army had to live off the land or be supplied from the cities in which they were quartered. After several years serving as a battlefield, the countryside was 'in so destitute a state after frequent devastation that it could provide little in the way of food'.

After three years of hard campaigning our soldier may have wondered what had induced him to sign up. He had marched up and down the Rhine and the Meuse, laid siege to forts and cities, fought and won a major battle (Strasbourg in AD 357), engaged in dozens of small skirmishes and when not marching and fighting had rebuilt destroyed forts and town walls. Yet Ammianus tells us that 'through all their meritorious service in dangerous and critical times, the troops, though worn out by their labours in Gaul, had received neither pay nor gratuity'. Furthermore, food continued to be scarce and when Julian 'took part of the seventeen days rations which the troops carried on their backs', to provision some rebuilt forts, the soldiers mutinied. Order was somehow restored and the campaign continued, but the mood of the troops must have remained precarious.

By AD 360, our soldier must have been a hardened veteran. He was by now at least a *semissalis*, since his unit must have received significant casualties over the previous four years. He was probably married, with his family following him from camp to camp and city to city. Then came an order for the *Heruli*, *Batavi*, *Petulantes* and *Celtae* to join the emperor in the East to take part in the Persian war. After all they had gone

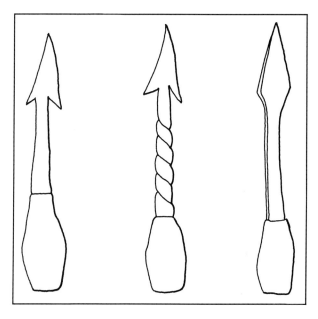

Above: A variety of iron, lead weighted, plumbatae heads. (after Völling)

A third century tavern scene. Being stationed in cities, the soldiers of the field army had the opportunity to spend what little hard cash they earned in such establishments. Julian's Gallic soldiers in Antioch are reported to have been drunk nearly every night. (Rheinisches Landesmuseum, Trier)

through it was too much: the troops mutinied again, but this time it was serious. In words attributed to a *Petulantes* soldier,

'We are to be driven off to the ends of the earth like condemned criminals while our nearest and dearest, whom we have set free from captivity after desperate fighting, again become slaves of the Alamanni.'

On hearing the complaint, Julian 'gave orders that they should start for the East with their families, and put at their disposal wagons of the public transport service'. This was not enough. The mutiny continued even after an assurance that no soldier would be forced to cross the Alps. Instead, the *Petulantes* and *Celtae* proclaimed Julian emperor by raising him up on one of their shields, while Maurus, the *draconarius* of the *Petulantes*, placed his gold neck torque on Julian's head as a diadem.

The posting to the East may have been the catalyst rather than the root cause of the mutiny, and Julian may have played on the soldiers' complaints to create the conditions for his elevation to emperor. Julian's promise to the *Petulantes* and *Celtae* gives us an idea of the true feelings of the men.

'I declare ... that no promotion, either civil or military, shall be given through unmerited patronage, and that no man who tries to pull strings on behalf of another shall escape without dishonour.'

Ammianus comments that 'the lower ranks who had gone without promotion or reward for a long time, were encouraged by this speech for better things'. This, along with a promised payment of five gold pieces and a pound of silver to each man, got the army marching behind Julian when he headed east to confront Constantius. We hear no more of the promise not to force the soldiers to cross the Alps. Perhaps the ringleaders of the mutiny had been bought off, or perhaps the soldiers were willing to head east if it meant payment of the promised money.

Life in a strange land

We can assume that our soldier marched eastward, probably reluctantly, but with a promise of a significant bounty ahead of him. His family would certainly have gone along, carried in the wagons of the baggage train. His rations and heavy equipment were also carried in wagons, leaving him relatively unencumbered. After several years of campaigning, there is a good chance he would have picked up a slave from enemy prisoners, and he too would have travelled with the baggage train.

By AD 362 we find our soldier in Antioch. He is in a strange land, living with his family in the house of an Antiochene who resents his presence. No one

A German warrior's grave goods. By the 5th century the weapons and equipment of Roman and German soldiers would have been virtually indistinguishable. Many of the so-called Goths who sacked Rome in AD 410 were in fact Roman deserters, while the majority of men in the ranks of 4th–5th century Roman units were Germans. (Copyright British Museum)

understands his pidgin Latin or German, and he and his family cannot understand Greek. The heat is oppressive, everything is dry and dusty, and the strange food does not agree with him. These circumstances had predictable results which are best described by Ammianus.

'The result was seen in the intemperate habits of the troops, who were gorged with meat and demoralised by a craving for drink, so that almost every day some of them were carried through the street to their quarters on the shoulders of passers-by after debauches in the temples which called for punishment rather than indulgence. Conspicuous in this respect were the Petulantes *and* Celtae, *whose indiscipline at this time passed all bounds.'*

On the march

In the spring of AD 363, marching orders were issued to the army, no doubt much to the relief of the citizens of Antioch and other cities that had borne the burden of quartering troops. Massive supply depots had been constructed in friendly territory along the route, so that the soldiers could draw rations and fodder along the way. An indication of the huge amount of supplies that had to be pre-positioned is provided by an incident in which a hayrick collapsed, killing 50 men.

The initial stages of the invasion would have resembled the march east from France. We cannot be certain that families would have gone along, but given the mutinous mood of the soldiers, they might have refused to march if it had meant leaving them behind. The *Strategikon* indicates that families would travel in enemy territory since the author cautions, 'The baggage train must be regarded as essential ... it includes the servants needed by the soldiers, their children and other members of their families. If their safety is not assured, the soldiers become distracted, hesitant and dispirited in battle.'

Once in enemy territory, caution would have increased. The *Strategikon* advises, 'The campsites should be fairly close, so that the infantry does not become worn out from marching long distances.' Furthermore, 'If the enemy are nearby, the soldiers should not leave their weapons in the wagons, but should carry them as they march along, so they may be ready to fight. In times of pressure they should march in the order of their battle formation, without any mixing of units or spreading out.'

The full disposition of the column as it crossed into Persia was recorded by Ammianus as having 1,500 skirmishers, advancing slowly and cautiously to the front and flanks, then the main body of infantry

Flavius Maximianus, a soldier of the auxilia palatina *in an elaborately decorated red tunic wearing what appears to be a bronze or gilded helmet of the type found at Intercisa. The helmet's plume is depicted in the same yellowish brown as the helmet itself. The dark patches at the front of the helmet are probably traditional eyebrow decorations. The shield design is similar but not identical to many* auxilia *patterns illustrated in the* Notitia Dignitatum. *Maximianus was perhaps in Sicily as part of the army gathered for Julian's aborted African expedition in 361. (Villa Maria catacomb, Syracuse)*

Most towns had amphitheatres where off-duty soldiers could enjoy the games. As town life declined many, like this one at Trier, were incorporated into the town's defensive walls. (Author's photo)

with several legions detached to clear the banks of the Euphrates on the right wing, while the cavalry covered the left. The column was well spaced out, reportedly to give an impression of greater size, but also in all likelihood to allow the men to march at an easy pace without having to keep slowing down or speeding up to conform to units in front of them. The entire column was ten miles long with 'the baggage, servants, non-combatant staff, and stores of every kind, placed between the two flanking divisions of regular troops'. Ships with extra supplies followed the army along the Euphrates.

The soldiers foraged as they went, and at this early stage of the campaign, food was plentiful. Hunting was good too, and we hear of herds of deer that were large enough to provide all the soldiers with fresh meat. Further supplies were gathered from the rich agricultural land through which the army marched. After gathering what they needed, the foraging parties burned the fields and villages. Ammianus tells us, 'Our warriors were glad to make use of the spoil won by their own hands ... and were delighted to have ample subsistence without having to draw on the supplies.'

Skirmishes and sieges

On any campaign, most of the action consisted of small skirmishes, which would involve only a few men in the advance, rear or flank guards. Full-scale battles were very rare, perhaps only one in an entire campaign. For the most part, our soldier in the ranks of the main body would trudge along day after day more concerned about the weather and food than the enemy. Quite probably he would be selected every once in a while to join a foraging or reconnaissance party. Such groups were usually formed by drawing several of the fitter men from each unit and equipping them for the task at hand, rather than assigning the job to a single unit.

Our man may have been one of the 'thousand light-armed men' who were sent in boats, under cover of night, to take the island fortress of Anatha by surprise. The assault party in their boats 'took station at suitable points to blockade the island, which a misty night enabled them to approach unseen'. The garrison was alerted, however, when the morning sun began to burn off the mist and the Romans were spotted by men drawing water from the river.

Most contact with the enemy would have occurred when a fortified town was reached. Often they could be induced to surrender or, if too strong, they would be bypassed as there was no time to settle down to a long siege. When an enemy fortification was reached that did not surrender but that could be assaulted, the army began siege operations. An example of this was the siege of Maozamalcha – a city, like the fort of Anatha, that was surrounded by the waters of the Euphrates.

The first step was to establish a secure base. To do this the soldiers built a proper fortified camp, protected by a double rampart. Fear of attack was justified when the Persians attacked the baggage train, although they were beaten off by the camp guards. Once established, patrols went out to scour the waterways in boats, to stop any enemy escaping from the city and to bring in prisoners for information. Our soldier may well have gone on some of these missions early in the operation, but before long the order was given for the infantry to prepare for an assault while the cavalry pillaged the countryside. The preparations are described by Ammianus.

'Duties were assigned and every man set about his allotted task with alacrity. Some were building high ramps, others filling ditches; elsewhere, long passages were driven into the bowels of the earth, and the artillerymen were setting up their engines, ready to burst out into deadly noise.'

For several days assaults were launched and beaten back. Casualties were probably heavy, caused not only by enemy action but also by accidents that occurred frequently. One such accident is recorded, when an engineer 'happened to be standing behind a scorpion (catapult) when a stone, carelessly fitted to its sling by an artilleryman, was hurled backwards. His breast was crushed, and he was thrown on his back and killed'.

Eventually one of the towers was demolished by a ram, and mines running under the fortifications were completed. Assaults were ordered on the walls to distract the enemy while troops broke out into the fortress through the mines. Our soldier could have been employed in either of these assaults. The assault through the mines was led by a soldier called Exsuperius of the *Victores*. The town was overrun by the Romans 'who in their fury destroyed all that came in their path without distinction of age or sex'.

Retreat and rearguard actions

Cities were besieged and captured, battles were won, but it probably did not take long for the men to realise they were not accomplishing much. The Persians retreated into the interior, burning their crops to deprive the Romans of supplies while at the same time constantly harassing them with hit and run attacks. The climate and terrain were unfamiliar to the men from the north, like our soldier, who formed the backbone of the army. One day a tornado hit, destroying the camp, and on another the river burst its banks.

A Pyrrhic victory at the Battle of Maranga did not achieve any strategic aims and the Romans 'were now destitute of food and tormented by pangs of

The General Stilicho, a Vandal, who led the Western armies of the early 5th century against the major Germanic migrations. (Monza Cathedral)

hunger. Crops and fodder had been burnt and men and beasts were at their last gasp, so a large part of the food carried by the baggage animals of the Tribunes and Counts was distributed to relieve the pressing needs of the rank and file'.

Shortly afterwards Julian was killed in a skirmish and the retreat began. The army was not allowed to withdraw unmolested, however. The Persians hovered on the flanks of the column, striking whenever an opportunity showed. Their elephants and heavily armoured cataphracts terrorised the Roman soldiers, this is evident from Ammianus' account of a rearguard action on the retreat.

'The Persians attacked with elephants in front. At first the smell and horror of their approach threw horses and men into confusion. But the Joviani *and* Herculiani *killed a few of the brutes and put up a stout resistance against the mail clad horse.'*

Out of food and deep in hostile territory, the Romans had no hope. Men dropped out of the line of march, only to be killed by the vigilant enemy. The column became more and more ragged, offering greater chances for hit and run attacks. Given these circumstances, the new emperor sued for peace. The remnants of the army were allowed to march home in exchange for the surrender of several important cities.

If our soldier of the *Petulantes* survived the expedition, he would now be a hardened, and probably embittered, veteran. After eight years hard campaigning, he would certainly have reached NCO rank, and we may wonder how many of the unit's original 500 actually returned to their Gallic homeland. We know that they did return to the West because the unit, along with the *Celtae*, is recorded campaigning along the Rhine 15 years later. By that time our soldier would either have been dead, maimed, retired after 20 years service, or have been one year away from full retirement with extra benefits – reward for 24 years service.

Taken from the tombstone of Lepontius, a soldier serving on the upper Rhine frontier in the 4th century, this carving gives us a crude impression of the *Gallo-Roman limitanei. His cockerel standard is perhaps a link with his Celtic past. (Musée Archeologique, Strasbourg)*

Campaigns of the 5th century

We do not have a Procopius or an Ammianus to give us a first-hand account of the life of the common soldier on campaign in the 5th century. We can, however, make certain observations. The soldier on campaign with Julian was clearly a fickle individual. He performed well enough when close to home, well fed and winning, but he had no great incentive to do more than necessary. When things went wrong, he did not hesitate to 'down tools' and extract fairly significant sums of money from his commander to keep going. By the 5th century, when large portions of the army were allied tribes, this situation must have been even more pronounced.

A Frank, for example, serving in the army of Aetius could reasonably be expected to perform well when defending his home against the Hunnic invasion of AD 451. But as soon as the threat was gone, he went home. There would have been no way Aetius could have persuaded him, or others like him, to

THE EXPERIENCE OF BATTLE

All the training, marching and logistical support had one ultimate goal: getting the soldier to the battlefield where he would meet and defeat the enemy at close quarters. As we have already seen, formal battle was not the soldier's most common experience. It was, however, his greatest test.

Preparation for battle

It was felt imperative that the soldier be well fed and rested prior to a battle. *Strategikon* advises that the 'foot soldiers should not be expected to march long distances in full armour' in order that they be fresh when they meet the enemy. This was on Julian's mind prior to the Battle of Strasbourg when he allegedly told his men,

'We are tired from our march . . . what are we to do when we meet the attack of the enemy hordes who will be rested and refreshed by food and drink? What strength shall we have to encounter them when we are worn out by hunger, thirst and toil? . . . I propose, therefore, that we set a watch and rest here, where we are protected by a rampart and ditch; then at first light, after an adequate allowance of sleep and food, let us, God willing, advance our eagles to triumph.'

Hunting scenes like this one provide the best examples of late Roman military dress. This man wears a red tunic with the usual round decorative patches, bare legs and long socks held up by thin laces in an elaborate cross-gartered pattern. Hunting is recommended in the Strategikon as a training exercise for soldiers. (Piazza Armeria, Sicily)

march to Italy the following year when the Huns switched targets. The end result was that Italy had to go undefended.

This reluctance of soldiers to serve beyond their local area became an immense problem. Therefore commanders formed their own private corps of retainers, known as *comitati* or *bucellarii*, who could be relied on to follow them wherever they went. Arthur's semi-legendary Knights of the Round Table are a famous example of such troops. Due to the need for mobility, these *bucellarii* were exclusively cavalry. The infantryman, even in units of the *comitatenses*, became little more than a militiaman who was only expected to protect the immediate area in which he was stationed. The Roman infantryman, only recently the backbone of the army, now rarely played a significant part on campaign.

Belisarius, too, preparing for battle against the Persians near Sura in AD 531 was concerned about his men going to fight on empty stomachs. It was Easter Saturday and the troops had been fasting; furthermore, Belisarius was afraid that the infantry might be worn out from the march to the battlefield. In both this case and at Strasbourg, the troops were seemingly so anxious for a fight that the general had to give in to them and lead them on in spite of their fatigue and hunger. This may well be nothing more than a literary device to make the victories that followed seem more remarkable, as one would assume that the common soldier would have been far more anxious to get a good meal and a rest than to hurry up and risk his life in combat.

According to Ammianus, one of the contributing factors to the Roman defeat at Adrianople in AD 378 was the fact that the soldiers had to march eight miles over rough ground under a burning sun before reaching the battlefield. Once there they had to stand in formation for several hours, without food or drink.

So let us assume that the soldier has rested, probably in a fortified camp. He would be woken before first light to get ready. This would entail a quick breakfast, probably of *bucellatum*, then he would put on his armour, gather his weapons and, in the grey light of dawn, form up with his unit for an inspection. The aim of this was to ensure that his equipment was complete and in as good repair as the campaign conditions would allow. At the same time, he would be reminded of his place in the formation and what was expected of him. The unit would then march out of the camp to its appointed position on the battlefield, which ideally would have been reconnoitred by the officers the night before while the men were resting. The men would march in their battle formation requiring only a 90° turn to change from march column to battle line.

The *Strategikon* describes the process of forming up for battle under ideal conditions. 'The divisions are drawn up in the battle line with intervals of one or two hundred feet between them, so they will not be crowded together while marching, but can still act in unison during battle and provide support for each other.' The general's standard would be posted in the centre of the battle line, and the first unit would form up there with the follow-on units forming to the right and left of it. The initial formation would be only four ranks deep 'since it is quicker and safer to close or tighten ranks than to open or broaden ... This makes our battleline more impressive to the enemy, and it also makes our soldiers more relaxed while marching'. It is worth noting that the wider the frontage of a unit, the harder it is for the troops to march, as it becomes increasingly difficult to maintain alignment.

Once in place, the soldiers were expected to remain absolutely quiet. The file closers 'should be instructed that if they hear so much as a whisper from one of their men, they should prod him with the butt of their spear'. The soldiers now had reached the point, best described in modern military slang, of 'hurry up and wait'. It could be many hours before they would be called on to play their part in the engagement, particularly if their unit was in the second line. In such a case the men would sit down

Vegetius says the pilum *was replaced by a weapon called the* spiculum. *He seems to equate it to the German* angon *which had a long iron head like this one found in France. (Copyright British Museum)*

Below: *The long spatha was the preferred side arm of the late Roman soldier. (Rheinisches Landesmuseum Bonn)*

29

and rest. 'If the weather is hot, let them take off their helmets and get some air,' advises the *Strategikon*. 'On such occasions they must not carry wine with them for it will only make them warm and dull their minds. Water, however, should be carried in the wagons and given to each individual who needs it as they remain in formation ... Only when the enemy gets close, should the men be called to attention, and they will be fresh and in good condition.'

The soldier in line of battle

The most common formation was the battle line or phalanx. This was, as Vegetius tells us, 'solely designed to repulse' an attack. It was used because infantry were usually being deployed defensively in this period, with cavalry providing the army's offensive capability. The line could be formed up in either four, eight or 16 ranks. The *Strategikon* says that fewer than four ranks did not have enough staying power and more than 16 added nothing to the unit's strength. As we saw above, it was easier to reduce frontage than expand, because of the accordion effect such a manoeuvre would have had on flanking units. It seems that in most cases an eight-rank formation was used, striking a balance between increasing staying power through depth and getting as many men as possible into action.

Arrian's *Against the Alans*, an actual battle order for a legion preparing to face cavalry, gives us a good idea of how such a formation would have looked:

'The legionaries will be formed in eight ranks and deployed in close order. The first four ranks will consist of men armed with the spear [probably *pilum*] *... The men of the first rank will present their spears at the approach of the enemy ... those of the second, third and fourth ranks will be in a position to throw their spears. They will be directed to aim their strikes accurately at the right time in order to knock down the horses and throw the riders ... The four ranks immediately behind will consist of men armed with the* lancea [a light spear]. *Behind these there will be a ninth rank composed of archers, those of the Numidians, Kyreneans, Bosporians and the Ituraeans.'*

Although from before our period, this order of battle is consistent with the rather confused descriptions of Vegetius. It also matches the *Strategikon*,

although a 16-rank formation is more common in this work. This may mean that the infantry of the later period needed increased depth to compensate for lower morale, or it may mean nothing more than that the author of the *Strategikon* plagiarised old Hellenistic manuals which used a 16-rank formation.

One thing that is clear in all descriptions is that the various ranks in a formation performed different tasks. The first four ranks were expected to do the real fighting and consequently were more heavily armed. The file closers in the rear rank had a supervisory role, while the men in the intervening ranks were to provide depth to the formation and throw light javelins over the heads of the front ranks. Attached archers from other units would be drawn up behind and also fire overhead. The *Strategikon* says that mail armour should ideally be provided for all men in the unit, but concedes that this may not be possible, in which case at least the first two and last ranks should have armour.

Vegetius has each man in the formation occupying a frontage of 1m and depth of 2m. This can be corroborated by a 3rd century shield found at Dura Europos which is about 1m wide. This frontage would have allowed the men to present a solid shield wall to the enemy, while the depth would have given room for the men to throw their javelins. Prior to contact, however, the ranks would move closer together, and the file closers 'should order those in the rear to close in forcefully on those to the front . . . if necessary to prevent some from hesitating and even holding back'.

The *cuneus*

The offensive formation used by the infantry of this period was the *cuneus*. It was a formation adopted from the Germans and was called the 'swine's head formation' by the soldiers. It was still used by the Vikings, centuries later, under the same name (*svyn-fylking* or swine array). The formation is described by Vegetius as 'a mass of men on foot, in a close formation, narrower in front, wider in the rear, that moves forward and breaks the ranks of the enemy'. The usual interpretation of this has been one or two men in the front rank with ever increasing numbers in succeeding ranks, forming a triangle. A Viking period description, for example, has two men in the front rank, three in the second and five in the third.

Such a neat triangular formation would have an advantage of being able to direct a high volume of fire to a single point. For this reason, as well as for ease of control, an arrowhead is a preferred formation of the 20th century infantry section. The Scythians and other highly mobile missile-armed cavalry also used a triangular formation, allowing the leader at the apex of the triangle to lead his men in all directions without the need for complicated drills. At the same time it provides maximum firepower to the front and flanks. This may be where Vegetius (a literary man, not a soldier) gets the idea that a triangular formation 'pierces the enemy line by a multitude of darts directed to one particular place'.

The *cuneus* of the German warrior and late Roman infantryman was clearly not designed for these reasons. It was a formation intended to deliver a decisive punch, breaking the enemy line through hand-to-hand combat. A triangular shaped formation would have failed miserably at this: the brave warrior all alone in the front rank would have been quickly

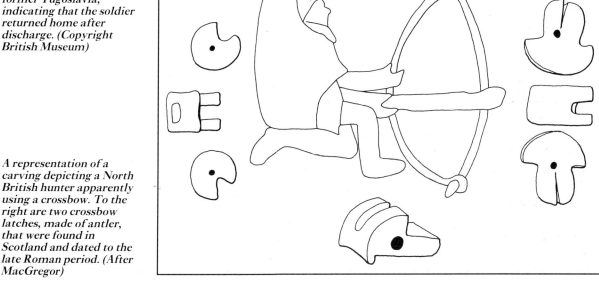

Left: A discharge diploma issued to an Illyrian soldier serving in Italy, 7 January AD 246. It was found in the former Yugoslavia, indicating that the soldier returned home after discharge. (Copyright British Museum)

A representation of a carving depicting a North British hunter apparently using a crossbow. To the right are two crossbow latches, made of antler, that were found in Scotland and dated to the late Roman period. (After MacGregor)

cut down, probably by enemy missiles before he even got close to their line. If he had made it into contact, he would have had to fight the enemy soldier directly to his front as well as those to his opponent's flanks. He would have had no support from his own men hanging back to keep the wedge shaped formation – unless of course these men rushed up to join him, in which case we might wonder why they had not been put there in the beginning. The German author Hans Delbrück sums this up nicely: 'No formation of a tactical body could be more foolish than this one. A group of men, no matter how firmly holding together, still remains the sum of the individuals, who, no doubt, push forward from the rear but cannot, like a sharpened piece of iron, concentrate the entire flanking pressure in a point or cutting edge.'

The real form of the *cuneus* can be found elsewhere. Tacitus, in his *Histories*, describes the formation as 'closely compressed on all sides and secure in front, rear and flank'. The *Strategikon* gives a similar description saying that the Germans attack in a formation that is 'even and dense'. This would indicate an attack column rather than a triangle. Taking a 400-man *auxilia* unit as an example, it might form a *cuneus* 16 men deep with a frontage of 25 men. Once the men in the column launched a charge, the neat alignment of the ranks and files would naturally be lost and the men in the centre, feeling more secure,

would surge forward, while those to the flanks might hang back. Just prior to contact, therefore, the *cuneus* could well have had a wedge-like appearance.

Both Vegetius and the *Strategikon* recommend that reserve units be deployed in *cuneus*. This makes sense if we accept that the formation was an attack column. Having a narrower frontage, it would be more manoevrable than a battle line and the depth of the column would give it the punch needed to break through an enemy formation or plug a gap in the line.

The *fulcum*

Another formation was the *fulcum* or *testudo*. The former name is possibly of German origin. The *Strategikon* describes it clearly.

'*The men in the front ranks close in until their shields are touching, completely covering their midsections almost to their ankles. The men standing behind them hold their shields above their heads, interlocking them with those of the men in front of them, covering their chests and faces, and in this way move to attack.*'

This formation was probably little more than a variation on the attack column, providing extra protection from enemy missile fire. The *Strategikon* recommends it when the front rank men do not have armour, and Ammianus provides an account of the

4th century infantrymen marching at ease, intermingled with the baggage train which is carrying their heavy equipment. (Arch of Constantine, Rome)

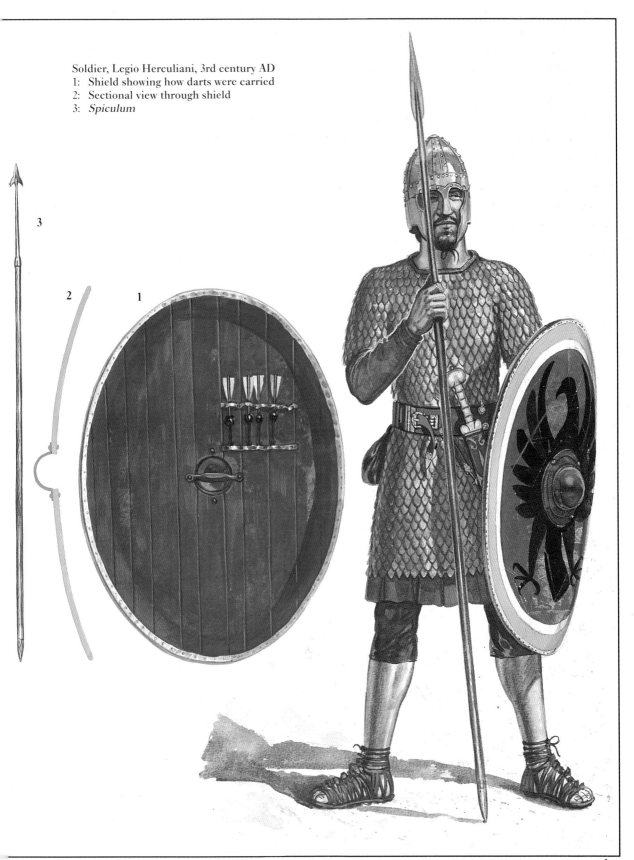

Soldier, Legio Herculiani, 3rd century AD
1: Shield showing how darts were carried
2: Sectional view through shield
3: *Spiculum*

A

Conscription, early 4th century AD

B

Archery training, 4th century AD

C

Soldiers on the march, 4th century AD

D

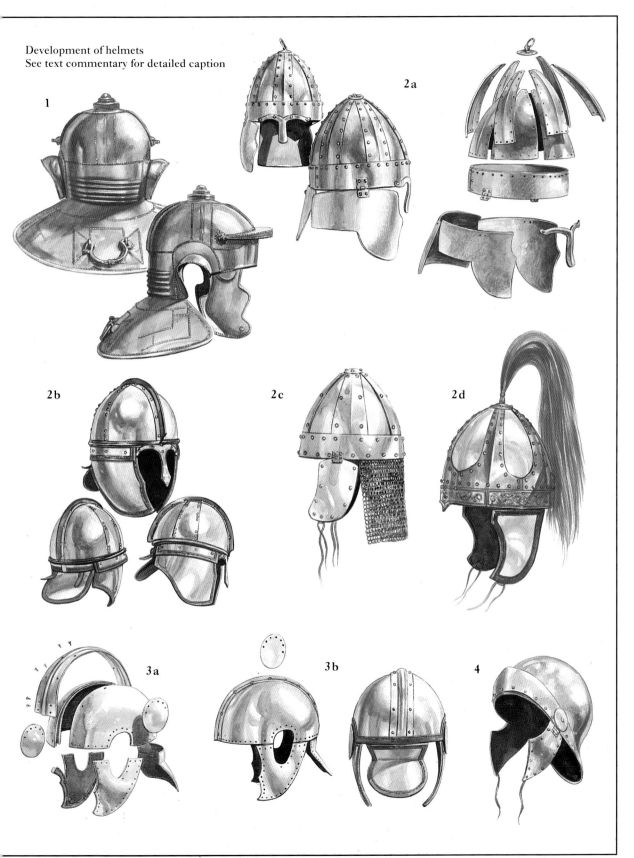

Development of helmets
See text commentary for detailed caption

1

2a

2b

2c

2d

3a

3b

4

E

Soldier, Auxilia Palatina, 4th century AD
1: Heavy equipment
2: Light equipment

F

Special operations, Rhine frontier, AD 357

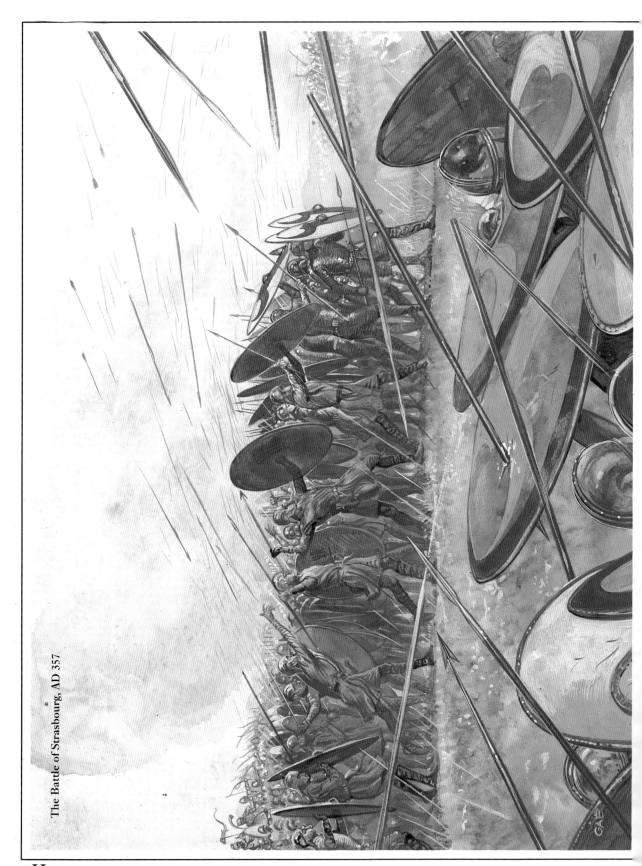

The Battle of Strasbourg, AD 357

H

Garrison life, Saxon shore, 5th century AD

I

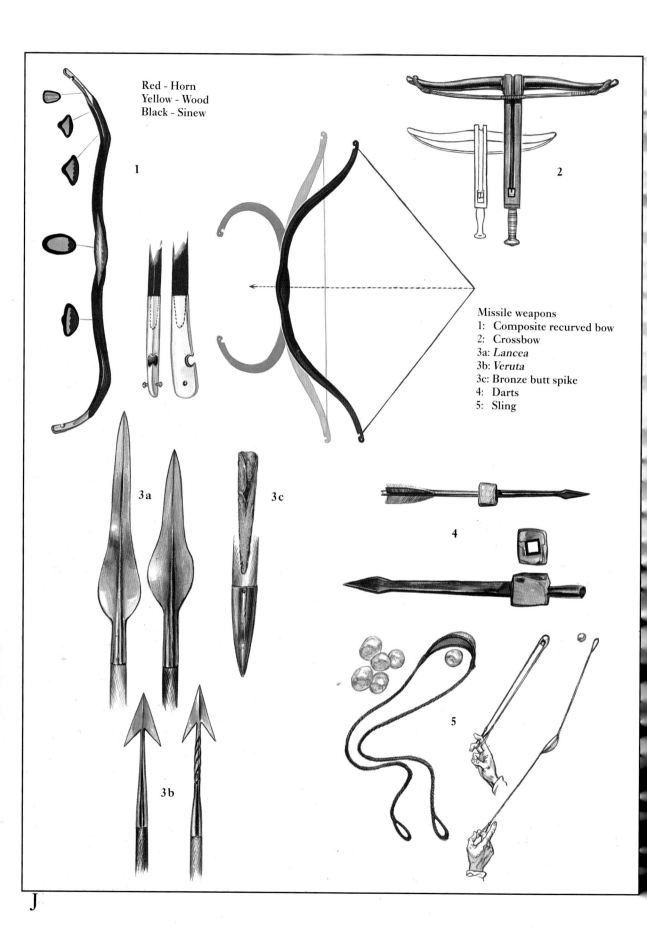

Red - Horn
Yellow - Wood
Black - Sinew

1

2

Missile weapons
1: Composite recurved bow
2: Crossbow
3a: *Lancea*
3b: *Veruta*
3c: Bronze butt spike
4: Darts
5: Sling

3a

3c

3b

4

5

J

The aftermath of battle, Campus Mauriacus, AD 451

K

East Roman soldier, Legio Quinta Macedonia, 5th-6th century AD
1: Military sandal
2: Scale armour, *(lorica squamata)*
3: Lamellar armour

L

men assaulting the city of Maozamalcha with 'interlocking shields which exactly covered our men like moving arches'. It was probably quite difficult to keep this formation up for any length of time, and certainly the men in it would have had to move very slowly. During the assault on Maozamalcha, for example, Ammianus says that the men's shields 'sometimes gaped apart under the strain of incessant motion'.

Skirmish formations

We have already observed that the soldier would be more likely to engage the enemy in a skirmish than a formal battle. Although the *Strategikon* advises against drawing men from different units for such actions, the accounts of Ammianus clearly show that, in the 4th century at least, this was the normal practice. If heavy infantrymen were to engage in a skirmish or to fight in rough terrain, the *Strategikon* says they 'should not have heavy armament such as helmets and mail coats' and they should be issued with smaller shields and short spears.

In such irregular warfare the men would naturally have fought individually rather than in formation. The *Strategikon* says that they 'ought not be drawn up in close order ... but in irregular groups, that is three or four armed with javelins and shields so they may protect themselves if necessary while hurling the javelin. They should also have one archer to provide covering fire for them'. The description of how they would operate is very similar to modern infantry tactics with small independent groups using terrain for cover and providing each other with mutual support.

'If something happens to the leading group, if, for example, they encounter resistance from the enemy or get bogged down in rough terrain, the groups behind them may move up to higher ground without being observed and come down upon the enemy's rear.'

Engaging the enemy

We can attempt to reconstruct how such formations and tactics might actually have been used from the writings of Ammianus and Procopius. We have already seen how a unit would deploy and wait, perhaps sitting down, for their part in the battle. Taking an example from an engagement with Gothic infantry in AD 377, we find a Roman battle line deployed and ready to meet the enemy charge. The Romans would probably have been called to attention with the enemy beyond maximum bow range – about 300 paces. Two ranks of archers, firing from behind the eighth rank, would probably open fire shortly after this. Firing at maximum range, at the dense

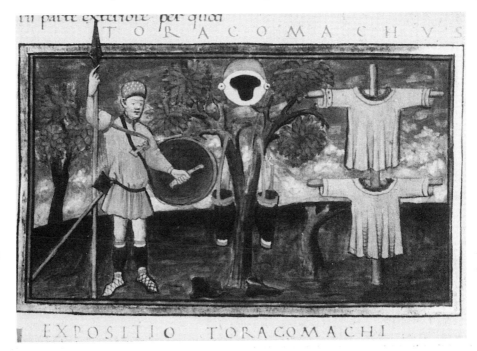

A late Roman soldier with his equipment from a medieval copy of a Roman original. He wears the ubiquitous fur pillbox, a red tunic, black leather belts and black leggings and shoes. His legs are bare. (Biblioteque Nationale, Paris)

This reconstruction of the famous Sutton Hoo helmet shows the high degree of 'cross cultural' exchange between Romans and Germans. The helmet is in fact a form of late Roman ridge helmet. The face guard would have severely restricted vision and would only have been suitable for a man fighting in a very close formation. Armourers who had produced such helmets for the Roman army probably had no difficulty modifying their style to suit the tastes of their new German masters. (Copyright British Museum)

target presented by the Gothic *cuneus*, the archers would be hoping to reduce the enemy's will to charge home rather than inflict serious casualties.

As the Goths drew closer to the Roman battle line, archery fire would become more effective, causing the advance to slow down and even halt before it came within close range. The two sides would now be between 50 and 100 metres apart. Casualties would have been relatively light, perhaps a few flesh wounds from arrows and a few faint-hearted men finding the opportunity to slip away. Ammianus describes the Romans as standing fast and remarks that no one 'strayed about or left the ranks'. They would still be well spaced out as the javelin volley would not yet have been delivered.

'When both sides had advanced cautiously and halted,' Ammianus goes on to tell us, 'the opposing warriors glared at each other with mutual ferocity. The Romans raised their morale by striking up their battle cry; this begins on a low note and swells to a loud roar, and goes by the native name of *barritus*.' The *barritus* was of German origin and no doubt the Goths would be doing the same thing. Both sides would be trying to intimidate each other with their battle cries and by clashing their spears on their shields. Tacitus, in the *Germania*, gives a detailed description of the *barritus* and its effect.

'They either terrify their foes or themselves become frightened, according to the noise they make on the battlefield ... What they particularly aim at is a harsh, intermittent roar; and they hold their shields in front of their mouths, so the sound is amplified into a deeper crescendo by the reverberation.'

Eventually, perhaps after only the briefest of checks, the Goths would begin moving forward again. When they were within 50 metres, the Roman archery fire might begin to cause actual casualties and then the front ranks would let loose with volleys of *plumbatae*. At this point one of three things could happen: the Goths could hesitate and begin to draw back; the Goths could look as if they were about to charge home, this might prove too much for the Romans' nerves, causing them to break; or with neither side intimidated, the Goths could close the last few paces and crash into the Roman formation. Ammianus tells us that the latter was the case and 'after an exchange of javelins and other missiles at long range, the opposing sides clashed and fought foot to foot in *twstudo* formation'.

Just prior to the clash the fifth, sixth and seventh ranks would loose a volley of javelins and then the file closers would push them forward to support the front ranks, while the archers continue to fire at high trajectory, dropping arrows on the rear of the enemy formation. According to the *Strategikon*, the men in the front two ranks, having thrown their darts, would crouch down, lock shields and 'fix their spears firmly in the ground, holding them inclined forward and straight outside their shields ... They also lean their shoulders and put their weight against the shields to resist any pressure from the enemy. The third man, who is standing nearly upright, and the fourth man, hold their spears like javelins, so when the foe gets close they can use them either for thrusting or for throwing and then draw their swords'.

Now a shoving match would ensue. Casualties would have been caused by the exchange of missile weapons by the men behind them; others would have fallen to the spears and swords of the enemy at the first clash. Now it was more a trial of stamina. As long as the soldier kept his footing and did not slip, he was unlikely to receive serious injury. In the tight press there can have been little room to use weapons effectively.

Eventually one side would begin to feel that things were not going well, either because they were being pushed back by a stronger formation or because of a sudden disaster, like a new enemy hitting them in the flank or rear. As morale began to crumble, men in the rear ranks would start slipping away, defying the efforts of the file closers to keep them in line. This

The city of Constantinople or New Rome, from a copy of the Notitia Dignitatum. *With the establishment of* *the new capital, the centre of power began to shift east. (Bodleian Library)*

would further weaken the formation, hastening their demise. Eventually the whole formation would give way and the real casualties would be inflicted. Ammianus vividly describes what happened to men who broke and ran. 'The fugitives on either side were pursued by the cavalry, who hacked at their heads and backs with all their strength, while at the same time men on foot hamstrung those who had got away but were checked by fright ... The whole field was strewn with corpses, among whom were some only half dead who still nursed a futile hope of survival.'

Tactics against cavalry

Facing a cavalry attack would have been much the same as facing a German infantry charge. In almost all cases the Roman foot soldiers would have held their ground to receive such a charge at the halt. A frontal cavalry charge on infantry, however, would have been a very rare thing, for the simple reason that while you can drive men on to do foolish things, you cannot do the same to horses. Modern recreations have found it nearly impossible to get horses to charge a shieldwall, particularly if the infantrymen are noisily clashing spears on their shields and raising the *barritus*. When this was attempted the horses stopped between five and ten metres from the enemy. Some would just halt, some would rear up, while others would turn sideways or step backwards. Riding them hard did nothing to help, and it was even worse if the infantry charged the horses.

The Persians discovered the same thing at the Battle of Sura in AD 531 when they went up against Belisarius' infantry, who, as we noted previously, were not exactly the same calibre as those of the 3rd and 4th centuries. It is worth reading Procopius' account of this engagement in full.

'The foot soldiers, and a very few of them, were fighting against the whole Persian cavalry. Nevertheless the enemy were not able either to rout them or in any other way overpower them. For standing shoulder to shoulder they kept themselves massed in a very small space, and *they formed with their shields a rigid, unyielding barricade, so that they shot at the Persians more conveniently than they were shot by them. Many a time after giving up, the Persians would advance against them, determined to break up and destroy their line, but they always retired again from the assault unsuccessful. For their horses, annoyed by the clashing of the shields, reared up and made confusion for themselves and their riders.'*

In the 4th century, when the infantry were more capable of aggressive action, Julian's soldiers quickly charged the Persian mounted archers on two recorded occasions. This accomplished two things: it reduced the amount of archery fire the Romans had to sustain and, as the modern tests confirmed, threw the enemy horses into confusion.

Relieving a besieged city. This 5th century wood carving from Egypt shows armoured infantrymen from two units (one with a shield design like Legio V Macedonia *) chasing away enemy cavalry and linking up with the garrison. The soldier on campaign might be involved in numerous sieges and small skirmishes but pitched battle would have been a fairly rare occurrence. (Museum für Spätantike und Byzantinische Kunst, Berlin)*

This floor mosaic shows a variation of the typical late Roman dress of loose, long sleeved undyed linen tunic, indigo decorative patches and bare legs. (Copyright British Museum)

As long as the infantry held their nerve, therefore, they had little or nothing to fear from cavalry. Far greater a danger was the cavalryman's mobility, that allowed him to get around the front or flanks of the infantry. The infamous defeat of the Roman army at Adrianople was brought about by such an attack by the Gothic cavalry on the Roman flank while they were frontally engaged.

Places to visit

Unfortunately there are very few places to visit that specifically relate to the late Roman period. Most Roman sites and museum collections concentrate on the High Imperial period which has left more artifacts to posterity. The following suggestions, however, are worth a trip:

Burg Linn Musium, Krefeld, Germany
Finds from Romano-Merovingian graves including a beautiful 5th century *spangenhelm* from an Illyrian fabrica.

Corrinium Museum, Cirencester, Gloucestershire

Ephesus, Turkey
The city was abandoned in the late Roman period because of plague. Probably the best preserved Roman ruins of the period.

Hadrian's Wall
Chesterholm, Cumbria; Chesters and Housesteads, Northumberland.

Istanbul, Turkey
Constantinople, the former Eastern Capital. Many sites of interest including city walls; military and archaeological museums; St Sophia; and the column of Theodosius.

Musee Archeologique, Strasbourg, France
Excellent Germanic collection from the period including a magnificent *spangenhelm*.

Painted House Museum, Dover Kent

Piercebridge, Durham
Roman fort from the 4th century.

Ravenna, Italy
The 5th century Western Capital, filled with late Roman and Ostrogothic sites. The many mosaics are particularly worth seeing at first hand.

Rijksmuseum, Leiden, Netherlands
Some magnificent late Roman helmets.

Rome
Of less interest for this period than Ravenna. However, the Arch of Constantine, Aurelian Walls and Vatican Museum, are worth a visit.

Römisch-Germanisches Museum, Cologne, Germany

Römisch-Germanisches Zentralmuseum, Mainz, Germany

Saxon shore forts
Burgh Castle, Norfolk; Cardiff Castle, S. Glamorgan; Richborough, Kent; Pevensey, East Sussex; Portchester Castle, Hants.

Trier Germany
One of the 4th century capitals. Imperial basilica and baths; Rheinisches Landesmuseum; Trier Städtisches Museum (for samples of late Roman clothing and applique patches).

York
Yorkshire Museum, city walls.

THE PLATES

A: *Soldier* Legio Herculiani *(3rd century AD)*
This man represents one of the many Illyrian soldiers that formed the core of the Roman armies in the chaotic 3rd century. He has seen some hard campaigning against the Palmyrans, Goths, Alamanni and numerous usurpers. Through his efforts and those of his countrymen, the Danube frontier has been secured and a semblance of order restored to the Empire.

The soldier's bronze scale armour or *lorica squamata* has replaced the more familiar segmented plate armour of the earlier legionaries. Iron ring mail might also have been worn, and a discovery of 3rd century *lorica segmentata* in Germany indicates that segmented armour had not yet completely died out along the western frontiers. He is armed with a *lancea*, a fairly light spear that could be thrown just before contact or retained for hand-to-hand fighting. The wood shaft has been painted to prevent rot, something that would not always have been possible under campaign conditions.

The man's shield design marks him as a member of the *Legio Herculiani*, one of the new elite, smaller legions. The *Herculiani* fought brigaded together with the *Jovianii* who had a similar shield design but in different colours. Vegetius says that the *Jovianii* and *Herculiani* were preferred by Diocletian above all other units, and that they were noted for their skill and dexterity with the five darts they carried in the hollow of their shields (**A1**). The shield is a large dished oval, based on an example found at Dura Europos. It is about 110cm high and 90cm wide, constructed of 1cm thick wood planks, covered and bound with leather. A hollow iron boss, that could also be bronze, covers the centre hand grip. **A2** shows a sectional view through the shield. Monuments and grave stones show that round shields were also in use at the time but that the traditional rectangular shield was on the way out.

Vegetius implies that the familiar heavy javelin or *pilum* had been replaced by the *spiculum* (**A3**). We cannot be sure whether this was the same weapon under a new name, or a new weapon. He describes the *spiculum* as a heavy javelin, 190cm long, with a fairly short iron head (less than 30cm), yet he equates it to the old *pilum* and Germanic weapons which had heads considerably longer than 30cm. This reconstruction gives Vegetius' description the benefit of the doubt.

B: Conscription (early 4th century AD)
In a foreshadowing of the feudal system, large landowners were expected to furnish recruits for the army from amongst their tenants. In this scene we see three reluctant young men being handed over to a recruiting party by the *bucellarii* or private retainers of a rich Gallo-Roman magnate. In a desperate attempt to avoid conscription, one of the men has amputated his thumb. Laws were passed, from the time of Constantine on, to try to stop recruits from doing this. In AD 368 Valentinian went so far as to instruct the Prefect of the Gauls that offenders should be burned alive. A few years later, Theodosius ordered that self-mutilated malingerers should serve regardless, and that landlords would have to produce two mutilated recruits in place of one sound man. With money in the right place, however, anything could be accomplished. This magnate has bribed the recruiting officer to accept men that do not meet the army's official standards of fitness, much to the consternation of the poor fellow who amputated his

This figure from a Greek 6th century mosaic depicts a soldier in a grey muscled cuirass, probably representing iron. Added protection is provided by pteruges at the shoulder and waist and additional leather apron like flaps at the waist. His helmet is a crude depiction of the Attic-style helmet. (Argos, Greece)

thumb. Naturally the landowner wants to keep his best men for himself, only passing on his least useful tenants to the army. Because a life in the army was so unpopular, recruits might be branded on the arm or hand to make desertion impossible.

The recruiters, who are probably Germans with no local sympathies, are in typical undress uniform for the period. Shields are not needed for this task, but the men are wearing helmets and carrying side arms in case of trouble. The landlord's *bucellarii* will help out if trouble does develop. These men might be ex-soldiers, even deserters, who are protected from the law by the magnate's power and thus owe their loyalty only to him. This practice of keeping private armies was technically illegal but became widespread during the Empire's disintegration, as it was the only means of providing islands of security in an ever increasing sea of chaos.

C: Archery training (4th century AD)
As the infantryman came to be employed more defensively, his ability to use longer-range missile weapons became critical. Archery training was parti-

cularly important and required a constant effort for the soldiers to achieve and maintain proficiency. Vegetius says, 'A third or a fourth of the recruits, those with talent, should be exercised at the post with wooden bows and training arrows ... the masters for this branch must be chosen with care and must apply themselves diligently to teach the men to hold the bow in a proper position, to bend it with strength, to keep the left hand steady, to draw the right with skill, to direct both the attention and the eye to the object.'

This scene shows several new recruits from the eastern provinces of the Empire undergoing archery training as described by Vegetius. The reference to 'wooden bows and training arrows' may indicate that expensive composite bows (**J**) were reserved for combat. The recruits have been issued with new linen tunics. They also wear the 'Pannonian leather caps' Vegetius claimed were obligatory 'so that thus constantly accustomed to having the head covered, the men would be less sensitive to the weight of the helmet'.

The master at arms or *campidoctor* is a long-service soldier. He, like the veterans looking on, has purchased his own clothing locally which therefore differs little from civilian dress. The military belt was often removed for comfort, as shown in several mosaics of the period.

The soldiers are being taught to shoot using the eastern thumb-draw with the aid of a thumb ring.

The *Strategikon* says that either this method or the western three-fingered pull were acceptable ways of teaching recruits to draw their bows. Since most archers were found in eastern units, it is quite probable that the thumb-draw was the most common.

D: Soldiers on the march (4th century AD)

The soldiers of the field army would have spent much of their life on the march. These troops had no permanent static bases; rather, they were quartered in the cities of the interior and deployed to wherever trouble developed. When they marched, everything went with them, including families, servants and all their personal belongings.

This scene, based on a relief from the Arch of Constantine, shows troops marching through relatively safe territory. Only spears and side arms are carried by the soldiers; all other equipment, such as shields, helmets and armour, follow in the nearby wagons. Cavalry outriders, also lightly equipped, screen the column, leaving the infantryman in the main body with little more to think about than the next rest stop.

When marching with enemy nearby, the *Strategikon* recommends that weapons should be carried by the troops rather than left in wagons and that 'troops on the march should not be mixed in or confused with the baggage train'. The fact that the *Strategikon*'s

Wondrous equipment such as this Balista Fulminalis was proposed by the anonymous author of a 4th century treatise as a solution to Rome's military troubles. It never saw the light of day. (Biblioteque Nationale, Paris)

author found it necessary to make such a statement may indicate that even in enemy territory, 6th century march discipline was not all it should have been. Whether this was also true 200 years earlier, we cannot be sure.

E: Development of helmets

This plate shows representative samples of the major helmet types worn by the late Roman soldier. In any unit a variety of styles might be found, as soldiers would have acquired their helmets at different times and places. Some would be content with mass-produced issued helmets, while others would have bought more elaborate versions that offered better protection. Many would have replaced old or battered helmets with battlefield salvage. The *fabricae* that produced helmets would not have churned out identical products throughout the Empire. Rather, they would have built on local traditions, perhaps producing *spangenhelms* in the Danube area and Attic-style helmets in Hellenistic regions.

The familiar 'Imperial-Gallic' and 'Imperial-Italic' style of helmet dropped out of use in the 3rd century. The last known example (**E1**) is a bronze helmet found at Niedermoerter, Germany. It is dated to the 3rd century and possibly belonged to a soldier of the XXX Legion.

The most common 3rd century helmet appears to have been on the *spangenhelm* type, of which the Der el-Medinah helmet (**E2a**) is a good example. These helmets probably originated amongst the Sarmatians of the Danube region. They were made up of several plates, usually six, held together in conical form by reinforcement bands. In their basic form they might be little more than a skull-cap, but the Roman versions usually had cheek pieces, neck guards and nose guards added as with the Berkasovo helmet (**E2b**). The fairly simple 3rd century Leiden helmet (**E2c**) is shown here with an added ring mail neck guard. **E2d** is a much later version found in an Alamannic grave in Alsace, showing the continuity of style throughout the period.

While the *spangenhelm* continued in use, particularly amongst the Germans, a new helmet style appeared in the 4th century. Known as 'ridge helmets', they are characterised by two bowls held together by a central ridge (**E3a**). They may have been influenced by Persian styles. Some could be

Mithras slaying the bull. Mithras was known as the 'soldiers' god' and the cult was extremely popular with men of all ranks, particularly in the 3rd and 4th centuries. By the 5th century, however, Christianity had completely taken hold throughout the Roman world, including the ranks of the army. (Ostia Antica, author's photograph)

quite elaborate and might have ben worn by officers or wealthy soldiers. Most, however, were very simple (**E3b**), suitable for mass production in the *fabricae* (state factories).

Although not confirmed by archaeological finds, another style of helmet, commonly depicted on reliefs and mosaics, was constructed with a single bowl, separate cheek pieces and brow reinforcement. They are often considered by archaeologists as a classical convention because they are similar to the Ancient Greek Attic style of helmet. However, they are different enough from the classical prototype to make this doubtful. **E4** is a reconstruction of an 'Attic' helmet from a 6th century Egyptian ivory.

F: Soldier, auxilia palatina *(4th century AD)*

The *auxilia palatina* formed the largest and most

Men like this 6th century Vandal or Alan from North Africa could be found fighting for or against the Romans. After their defeat by Belisarius, several units of Vandals were raised and sent to the Persian front. (Copyright British Museum)

important part of the 4th century armies, particularly in the West. A soldier who belonged to such a unit, might fight in the line of battle, equipped as the main figure, or be employed on special operations calling for lighter equipment, as in the inset. He is most likely a Gallo-Roman or a German.

The main figure wears a plumed version of the ridge helmet. While many monumental and literary sources indicate that plumes were common, archaeological finds have yet to produce a method of attaching them to the helmet. Plumes were usually of stiffened horsehair, and the most common colours seem to have been red, yellow, white and black. There is some indication that they matched shield colours to help unit identification.

The ring mail armour depicted is conjectural, representing what might have been the model for artists of the period who depicted soldiers in classical muscled cuirasses. Such depictions usually show swords worn from baldrics over the shoulder, without a waist belt. Presumably the waist belt, which was a universal item of military dress, was worn under the armour.

The shield is a large flat oval painted with a design shown on a mid 4th century fresco from Syracuse. The design does not exactly match any in the *Notitia Dignitatum* but it is similar to those of the *Cornuti Seniores*, *Marcomanni Seniores* or *Constantiani* and might be an earlier version of one of them.

The inset shows how the soldier would be equipped when sent on a patrol, foraging expedition or similar task. His helmet and armour have been left behind and he has replaced his spear with a light javelin. He might also carry several darts or a sling. The *Strategikon* suggests that troops sent on such missions might be given smaller, lighter shields. While this would make good tactical sense, it would have been very difficult logistically. It is, therefore, unlikely to have been normal practice. Specialised light infantry units, however, probably carried smaller shields all the time.

G: Special operations, Rhine frontier (AD 357)
Much, perhaps most, of the soldier's combat experience would have been gained in small engagements and skirmishes rather than pitched battle. This scene recreates a description by Ammianus Marcellinus of such an action that took place in the upper Rhine

valley prior to the Battle of Strasbourg. The Rhine in this region is characterised by numerous small shallow waterways dotted with islands. The Alamanni, who had settled to the west of the Rhine, sought refuge on these islands when the Roman army approached. Ammianus tells us how the Romans dealt with them.

'Julian, learning from some scouts who had just been captured that since it was now high summer the river was fordable, encouraged a body of light-armed auxiliaries under Bainobaudes, the Tribune of the Cornuti, *to attempt an exploit which would bring them renown if luck was on their side. Wading through the shallows and at times supporting themselves on their shields and swimming, they reached a nearby island where they landed and slaughtered everyone they found like sheep, without distinction of age or sex. Then finding some empty boats, they went on in them, rickety though they were, and forced their way through a number of similar places. Finally, when they were sick of the slaughter, they all returned safe with a rich haul of loot, though some was carried off by the force of the stream.'*

H: The Battle of Strasbourg (AD 357)

The men involved in the operation on the Rhine, shown in the previous plate, found themselves a short while later in formal battle. Once again Ammianus Marcellinus sets the scene.

'The Cornuti *and* Bracchiati, *veterans long experienced in war, intimidated the enemy by their bearing and put all their strength into their famous war-cry ... Volleys of javelins flew hissing through the air on both sides. A uniform cloud of dust arose and obscured the field, in which arms were hurtling against arms and bodies against bodies ... The hail of darts and javelins and the volleys of iron tipped arrows did not slacken, although blade was clashing on blade in hand to hand combat, breastplates were split asunder by sword blows, and wounded men who still had some blood left rose from the ground to attempt some further exploit.'*

This scene captures the moment just before contact. The two sides are trying to intimidate each other and to build up courage. The front ranks are closed up ready for the clash, the rear ranks are throwing javelins and the whole formation is suppor-

This soldier is depicted on a 7th century Alamannic silver plate. His deliberate classical appearance is obviously an artistic convention, but he may represent the Gallo-Roman soldiers cut off by German settlements. According to Procopius these people carried their dress and traditions into the 6th century. (Musée Archéologique, Strasbourg)

ted by a unit of archers (*Sagittarii Nervii*) firing overhead. This missile support probably produces more of a morale effect rather than causing a significant number of casualties.

The Tribune, Bainobaudes – who commanded the operation shown in **G** – keeps an eye on his formation from the rear. He will soon order the trumpeter to blow a signal for the entire formation to close up ready for the shock of contact. When this happens, the NCOs in the rear rank will forcibly push the men forward. Already they are prodding a few shirkers back into line. The most reliable men are in the first few ranks. It is they who will bear the brunt of the fighting, and consequently they are better equipped. The rear ranks who primarily provide depth and support have a lesser need of armour and if there is not enough to go around, will go without.

I: Garrison life, Saxon Shore (5th century AD)

While the men of the field army led a life on the move, the troops of the *limitanei* stayed in one place, providing a hereditary garrison for various frontier posts. These troops would have been far more integrated into the local community than the *palatini* or *comitatenses*. Since their profession was hereditary, and land was granted on discharge, some soldiers would have had fairly extensive family estates which they would have inherited from their forefathers.

When the troops of the field army were withdrawn from Britain at the beginning of the 5th century, it is highly unlikely that many of the garrison troops would have gone with them. By this time, the loyalty of the *limitanei* was first to the land, then to the army. If an order to move from Gaul to the East caused a mutiny in Julian's 4th century field army, a

Armoured infantryman on escort duties, taken from a 6th century Egyptian ivory. They can be identified by their shields as men of Legio V Macedonia. *By this time such men would have played a secondary role in warfare; the army's main offensive arm was made up of armoured horse-archers like the man in the centre. (Rheinisches Landesmuseum, Trier)*

similar order certainly would not have been obeyed by 5th century *limitanei*. That various Roman units continued functioning long after the disappearance of Roman authority is confirmed by Procopius, who says that Roman soldiers stationed on the frontiers of Gaul maintained their military traditions through to his day (mid 6th century) and could even be 'recognised as belonging to the legions they were assigned when they served in ancient times'.

This scene, set at Anderita (modern Pevensey), assumes a continuity of military activity through the 5th century. Some off-duty soldiers take a break from working to gossip with friends returning from a watch along the coast, while in the background their families work on the land. The men belong to the *Numerus Abulcorum* listed in the *Notitia Dignitatum* as being stationed at Anderita. They might be German settlers. Their equipment is simple but fairly uniform on the assumption that at a small static post, there would be only one source of supply. The equipment of the soldiers on duty is based on a later Alamannic source showing a very Roman looking soldier – perhaps one of the men described by Procopius. There is a slim possibility that they have armour in the fort, but if so it would be saved for battle.

The fate of the garrison of Anderita is described

by the entry for AD 491 in the Anglo-Saxon Chronicle. 'In this year Aelle and Cissa besieged Andredesceaster and slew all the inhabitants; there was not even one Briton left alive there.'

J: Missile weapons
J1: Composite recurved bow
This bow, of Eastern origin, was the most common type used by Roman troops, although simple longbows might possibly have been used in the West. The bow is made up of layers of horn, wood and sinew. The core is wood with a layer of horn on the inside, and sinew on the outside. The tips, where the string was notched, were reinforced with bone or antler. These bows probably had a maximum range, with some hope of penetration, of about 200–300 metres.

J2: Crossbow
Vegetius implies that crossbows, which he calls *arcubalistae*, were in fairly common use. They were possibly carried by the *legiones balistarii*, mentioned by Ammianus and listed in the *Notitia Dignitatum*. The *Strategikon* describes the crossbow (*solenarion*) as a light infantry weapon which fires short arrows a great distance.

J3: Spears and javelins
The *lancea* (**J3a**) was the infantryman's primary weapon. It was light enough to be thrown just prior to contact or could be retained for use in hand-to-hand combat. Javelins (**J3b**) known as *veruta* were a major part of the Roman infantryman's arsenal. They might be carried instead of a *lancea* by rear ranks in a battle formation and certainly would have been used when skirmishing. They were used at quite close quarters since although they could be thrown as far as 30m, accurate effective range was closer to 10m. Javelins ranged from 80–120cm long and weighed 300–600g. They had a small iron tip (often barbed) and bronze butt spike (**J3c**). When armed with javelins, the soldier probably carried at least 2 or 3.

J4: Darts
The *plumbatae* or *mattiobarbuli* had iron, lead-weighted heads averaging 10–20cm long, with a wooden flighted shaft of about the same length. They weighed about 100–200g. Being light and easy to carry, these weapons would have given a heavily

A fragment of a 4th century Roman helmet found together with link mail that probably provided a neck guard for the original wearer. (St Irminen, Trier)

armed foot soldier the ability to engage a more mobile target. They would have outranged common javelins, and would have been easier to throw while standing still in a tight formation. On the other hand they would have been fairly complicated and expensive to produce.

J5: Sling
This simplest of missile weapons was recommended by Vegetius as a secondary weapon for infantrymen engaged in skirmishes and sieges. Since it would have required quite a bit of practice to become proficient with the weapon, we cannot be sure if Vegetius' advice was followed. The *Funditores* listed in the *Notitia Dignitatum*, as part of the Syrian field army, might have been a specialised unit of slingers.

K: The aftermath of battle, Campus Mauriacus (AD 451)
In AD 451, Aetius' coalition of Romans, Franks, Alans and Visigoths fought Attila's equally diverse army of Huns, Ostrogoths and Gepids to a standstill on the Plains of Champagne in northern France. There probably was not a true Roman anywhere in Aetius' army; even those nominally Roman units would have

The Saxon Shore fort of Anderita (Pevensey) was home to the Numerus Abulcorum in the 4th and 5th centuries. It was attacked and captured by Saxons in AD 491. (Author's photograph)

been composed of German military settlers. The quality of these troops, particularly the infantry, was probably very low. In an allegorical speech to his men (reported by a Gothic historian) Attila is supposed to have said, 'The Romans are poor soldiers, keeping together in rank and file. They are contemptible, the only worthy enemies are the Alans and the Visigoths.'

The battle was very hard fought. It lasted all day with enormous casualties on both sides but nightfall saw the Romans in possession of the field. This scene shows some of the Roman and Frankish victors scouring the battlefield – helping their wounded comrades; finishing off those of the enemy; and more importantly searching for loot. One poorly equipped Roman has found a magnificent lamellar helmet that belonged to a Gepid nobleman. He does not hesitate to replace his old battered ridge helmet with his new find.

L: East Roman soldier, Legio Quinta Macedonia (5th–6th century AD)

This soldier traces a military tradition back several centuries to the old V Legion. In the earlier part of

the 5th century his unit belonged to the Syrian field army; by the time of Justinian they were part of the Egyptian garrison. His equipment represents the best available to infantrymen of this period. Many other soldiers, particularly in the 5th century West, would have been much more poorly equipped. He wears an Attic-style helmet, which is the most commonly depicted form for this period in the East, although *spangenhelms* and ridge helmets were probably still worn. His mail armour (*lorica hamata*) provides a flexible and comfortable form of protection. The split in the skirt would have facilitated movement and, since Procopius mentions mounting infantry on captured horses, would have enabled the man to ride.

L1: Military sandal

The usual footwear of the late Roman soldier was a fairly closed sandal that derived from Celtic and Germanic styles rather than the more familiar Italian *caligae*. Some 6th century sources seem to depict boots being worn. This seems a rather expensive and impractical form of footwear for an infantryman, and they may actually be intended to represent stockings or gaiters. The *Strategikon* specifically states, 'Boots or greaves are not required, for they are unsuitable for marching.'

L2: Scale armour

Scale armour (*lorica squamata*) continued to be worn, often alongside mail. Many examples of scales that have been found are poorly finished, suggesting mass production by poor quality armourers. Scales were linked together with wire and attached in rows to a lace, which in turn was sewed to a fairly stiff linen backing. Each row overlapped the one below it by about a third. The neck opening was covered by a leather band to protect the wearer against the rough, sharp edges of the scales. *Lorica squamata* would have been cheaper and easier to produce than mail but it was nothing like as flexible. As a result, additional protection was sometimes provided by leather strips (*pteruges*) at the shoulders and waist.

L3: Lamellar armour

Another alternative form of armour was made of narrow vertical plates (*lamellae*), which were laced together horizontally and vertically. Lamellar probably had its origin in the Asiatic east, and it remained popular in the Byzantine Empire long after this period. Like scale, lamellar would have been a fairly inflexible form of armour requiring additional *pteruges* at the waist and shoulders. Lamellar, however, does not seem to have been worn by the rank and file infantrymen of this period, expense perhaps limiting it to officers and some heavy cavalrymen.

GLOSSARY

Alamanni A confederation of German tribes who were one of Rome's main opponents in this period.

Angon A German heavy javelin with long iron head. A cheap version of the old Roman *pilum*.

Auxilia A new type of unit created at the end of the 3rd century with a full strength of about 500 men. All belonged to the elite *palatini*.

Barritus A German war cry adopted by the Romans.

Bucellarii Personal retainers of magnates and warlords.

Bucellatum Dried biscuit or hard tack which formed part of the soldier's field rations.

Campidoctor A unit's master at arms or drill instructor.

Comitatenses Line troops of the mobile field army.

Cuneus An attack column used by German and Roman infantry. Often mistakenly identified as a wedge.

Draconarius A unit's standard bearer who carries the windsock style dragon standard (*draco*).

Fabricae State run arms factories.

Federates (*foederati*) Foreign troops serving in the Roman army under their own leaders.

Fulcum A 6th century name for the *testudo* formation.

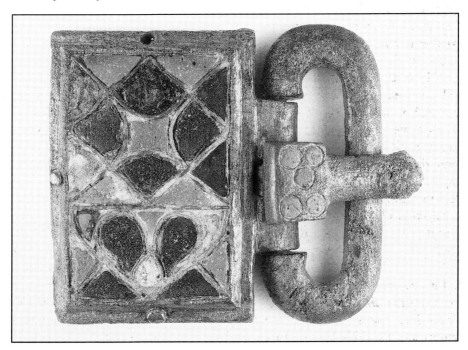

This 5th century German-style belt buckle was found in Egypt, it must have belonged to a German soldier serving in the Roman army a long way from home. (Copyright British Museum)

Illyria A Roman province roughly equating to the former Yugoslavia of the 20th century. It was a major source of recruits, particularly in the 3rd century.

Isauria A mountainous area of Asia Minor and source of many 6th century infantry recruits.

Lancea A light spear that could either be thrown or retained for hand-to-hand combat. Probably the preferred weapon of the late Roman infantryman.

Legions The traditional name for units of Roman citizen infantry. During this period their composition and battlefield role was virtually indistinguishable from the *auxilia*. They had an establishment strength of up to 1,200 men.

Limitanei Static frontier troops.

Lorica Armour. Types used in this period include: *segmentata* (segmented plate armour); *hamata* (mail); *squamata* (scale) and *lamellar* (small vertical iron plates).

Murci Draft dodgers who cut off their thumbs to evade military service.

Notitia Dignitatum A list of offices of the late Roman administration; includes a fairly complete listing of army units and shield designs.

Palatini Elite troops of the mobile field army.

Pedes An ordinary foot soldier.

Pilum A heavy javelin with long iron head. It had fallen out of use by this time.

Plumbatae (also **mattiobarbuli**) Lead weighted darts.

Pseudocomitatenses *Limitanei* transferred to the field army.

Semissalis An experienced soldier, roughly equivalent to a modern lance corporal.

Spangenhelm A conical segmented helmet of Danubian origin worn throughout this period.

Spatha A fairly long sword that was the favoured side arm of the period.

Soldiers attending the Emperor Justinian. Their lack of uniformity is interesting. Spear shafts have been elaborately painted. (San Vitale, Ravenna)

Spiculum A name given to a later form of heavy javelin. Perhaps similar to the *pilum* and *angon* but with a smaller point.

Strategikon A military manual written at the end of the 6th century.

Testudo A Roman formation in which the soldiers completely cover their front, sides and heads with their shields. Also called *fulcum*.

Tiro A recruit.

Vegetius Flavius Vegetius Renatus. A 5th century writer who produced a military treatise lamenting the demise of the classical heavy legions and urging improvements in training and equipment.

Verutum A light javelin.

BIBLIOGRAPHY

Primary sources

Arrian, *Against the Alans.*

Tacitus, *The Histories.*
    The Germania.

Procopius of Caesarea, *History of the Wars.*

Ammianus Marcellinus, *The Histories.*

Mauricius, *The Strategikon.*

Notitia Dignitatum.

Vegetius, *The Art of War.*

Secondary sources

Barker, Phil, *The Armies & Enemies of Imperial Rome* (Worthing, 1981).

Bachrach, Bernard S., *A History of the Alans in the West* (Minneapolis, 1973).

Bona, Istvan, *The Dawn of the Dark Ages* (Budapest, 1976).

Burns, Thomas, *A History of the Ostrogoths* (Bloomington, Indiana, 1984).

Bury, J. B., *History of The Later Roman Empire* (New York, 1958).

Christlein, Rainer, *Die Alamannen* (Stuttgart, 1978).

Coulston, J. C. N., 'Late Roman Armour, 3rd–6th Centuries AD', *Journal of Roman Military Equipment Studies I* (London, 1990).

Christodoulou, Dimitris, 'Byzantine Complexities II, Unit Organisation and Nomenclature (500-600 AD)', *Slingshot, Vol 147* (1990).

Dennis, George T., 'Flies, Mice and the Byzantine

Gravestone of a 3rd century soldier with his slave. On campaign the soldier would be followed by his family and personal belongings which often included slaves. (Römisch-Germanisches Museum, Cologne)

Crossbow', *Byzantine and Modern Greek Studies 7* (1981).

Delbrück, Hans, *Geschichte der Kriegskunst im Rahmen der Politischen Geschichte* (Berlin, 1921).

Dupuy & Dupuy, *The Encyclopaedia of Military History* (New York, 1970).

Ferrill, Arthur, *The Fall of the Roman Empire, the Military Explanation* (London, 1986).

Gilbert, J. M., 'Crossbows on Pictish Stones', & A. MacGregor, 'Two Antler Crossbow Nuts', *Proceedings of the Society of Antiquaries of Scotland* (1975–6).

Gibbon, Edward, *The Decline and Fall of the Roman Empire* (New York, Modern Library, no date).

Gordon, C. D., *The Age of Attila* (Toronto, 1966).

Haldon, J. F., 'The Byzantine Crossbow', *University of Birmingham Historical Journal, Vol XII* (1970).

This scene from a 5th century ivory shows soldiers in typical undress uniform, sleeping on guard duty. Such an offence would have been severely punished in earlier times. (Villa Sforza, Milan)

Harrison, Derek, 'Later Romans: Variations on a Theme', *Slingshot, Vol 94* (1981).

Hoffman, Dietrich, *Das Spaetrömische Bewegungsheer und die Notitia Dignitatum* (Dusseldorf, 1970).

James, Simon, 'Evidence from Dura Europos for the Origins of Late Roman Helmets', *Revue d'Art Oriental et d'Archeologie* (Paris, 1986).

Jones, A. H. M., *The Later Roman Empire* (Oklahoma University Press, 1964).

Johnson, Stephen, *Later Roman Britain* (Norfolk, 1980).

Junkelmann, Marcus, *Die Reiter Roms, 3 Vols* (Mainz, 1992).

Keegan, John, *The Face of Battle* (London, 1976).

Lot, Ferdinand, *The End of the Ancient World and the Beginnings of the Middle Ages* (Trans., New York, 1961).

Luttwak, Edward N., *The Grand Strategy of the Roman Empire* (London, 1976).

Maenchen-Helfen, Otto J., *The World of the Huns* (Los Angeles, 1973).

Moss, J. R., 'The Effects of the Policies of Aetius on the History of Western Europe', *Historia LXXII* (1973).

Nauerth, Claudia, *Die Koptischen Textilien der Sammlung Wilhelm Rautenstrauch im Städtischen Museum Simeonstift Trier* (Trier, 1989).

du Picq, Ardant, *Battle Studies* (Trans., Harrisburg, 1947).

Taeckholm, Ulf, 'Aetius and the Battle on the Catalaunian Fields', *Opuscula Romana VII* (1969).

Theocharidis, Ploutarchos L., 'Late Roman and Early Byzantine Helmets', *Proceedings of the 1st International Symposium on Everyday Life in Byzantium* (Athens, 1989). With notes from Dimitris Christodoulou.

Davis Randers-Pehrson, Justine, *Barbarians & Romans* (Kent, 1983).

Voelling, Thomas, *Plumbata-Mattiobarbulus-Marzobandoulon, Bemerkungen zu einem Waffenfund aus Olympia* (no date).

Wallace-Hadrill, J. M., *The Barbarian West* (New York, 1961).

INDEX

Figures in **bold** refer to illustrations

COMPANION SERIES FROM OSPREY

MEN-AT-ARMS

An unrivalled source of information on the organization, uniforms and equipment of the world's fighting men, past and present. The series covers hundreds of subjects spanning 5,000 years of history. Each 48-page book includes concise texts packed with specific information, some 40 photos, maps and diagrams, and eight color plates of uniformed figures.

ELITE

Detailed information on the uniforms and insignia of the world's most famous military forces. Each 64-page book contains some 50 photographs and diagrams, and 12 pages of full-color artwork.

NEW VANGUARD

Comprehensive histories of the design, development and operational use of the world's armored vehicles and artillery. Each 48-page book contains eight pages of full-color artwork including a detailed cutaway.

CAMPAIGN

Concise, authoritative accounts of history's decisive military encounters. Each 96-page book contains over 90 illustrations including maps, orders of battle, color plates, and three-dimensional battle maps.

ORDER OF BATTLE

The most detailed information ever published on the units which fought history's great battles. Each 96-page book contains comprehensive organization diagrams supported by ultra-detailed color maps. Each title also includes a large fold-out base map.

AIRCRAFT OF THE ACES

Focuses exclusively on the elite pilots of major air campaigns, and includes unique interviews with surviving aces sourced specifically for each volume. Each 96-page volume contains up to 40 specially commissioned artworks, unit listings, new scale plans and the best archival photography available.

COMBAT AIRCRAFT

Technical information from the world's leading aviation writers on the aircraft types flown. Each 96-page volume contains up to 40 specially commissioned artworks, unit listings, new scale plans and the best archival photography available.